Teamwork in the Management of Emotional and Behavioural Difficulties

Developing Peer Support Systems for Teachers in Mainstream and Special Schools

Fran Hill and Lynne Parsons

David Fulton Publishers
London

David Fulton Publishers Ltd
The Chiswick Centre, 414 Chiswick High Road, London W4 5TF
www.fultonpublishers.co.uk

First published in Great Britain in 2000 by David Fulton Publishers

Note: The rights of Fran Hill and Lynne Parsons to be identified as the authors
of this work have been asserted by them in accordance with the Copyright,
Designs and Patents Act 1988.

David Fulton Publishers is a division of Granada Learning Limited, part of
Granada plc.

British Library Cataloguing in Publication Data
A catalogue record for this book is available from the British Library.

ISBN 1-85346-619-0

Typeset by FSH Print and Production Ltd, London
Printed and bound in Great Britain

Acknowledgements

This book is based on GEST funded work carried out with schools in Oxfordshire during 1997–8. Two members of staff from each of the schools that took part attended a course over a six week period. Workshops were held weekly and each session lasted 2.5 hours.

This work developed out of a pilot project entitled 'The Challenging Child – A Problem Solving Approach', and we would like to thank the course participants of the following schools:

Drayton School, Banbury
Cropredy Primary School, Banbury
Hardwick Primary School, Banbury
Neithrop Infants School, Banbury
Neithrop Junior School, Banbury
William Morris Primary School, Banbury
Cooper School, Bicester
Donnington Middle School, Oxford
Marston Middle School, Oxford
Wesley Green Middle School, Oxford
Milham Ford School, Oxford
St Augustine's School, Oxford
The Cherwell School, Oxford.

We would also like to thank our long suffering families and John Owens at the publishers who kept us on task and without whose support and encouragement this book may never have reached a conclusion.

Introduction

'This book is based on research and practice carried out with individual schools and partnerships of schools in Oxfordshire over several years. The culmination of this work resulted in a bid submitted to the DfEE in October 1996 for GEST funding to support pupils with emotional and behavioural difficulties, and the staff who work with them. The project was entitled 'Promoting Positive Behaviour in Schools – Developing Peer Support for Teachers'. The concept of this particular bid was based on one of the recommendations of the Elton Report: 'Head teachers should promote the development of both management support and peer support within the staff team, and the professional development of its members.' (Elton Report 1989, Recommendation 19 (DES)).

Each participating school was asked to send two members of staff to take part in weekly workshops over a six week period. In total this amounted to between 16–18 hours of training. It was important that at least one of the pair had managerial responsibility in order to cascade the work back to the whole school staff. Prior to the workshops taking place a complete needs analysis of each participating school was undertaken. The questionnaires, surveys and observation schedules used to do this work are in Part One of the book.

Each of the subsequent six workshops consisted of two halves. The first part was devoted to aspects of professional development. The content related specifically to the issues that had arisen as a result of the needs analysis in the various schools taking part. Over and above this participants often raised areas of concern relating to the case studies presented, and this too formed part of the professional development element of the workshops. Some of these topics are in Part Two of the book, but schools setting up regular peer support meetings may choose to discuss a range of issues, all of which might impact on behaviour in school. This could include teaching and learning styles, differentiation, avoiding confrontation and anger management or supporting pupils to develop effective learning skills. Schools should make their own decisions about which topics and activities need further exploration within their own establishments. The purpose of this part of the workshops was to encourage and emphasise the notion of schools as learning organisations where the continuing professional development of the staff made a significant contribution to effective schooling. This part of the workshop encouraged experiential learning and participants undertook a variety of activities and exercises to rehearse and practise the skills being discussed.

The second half of the peer support meeting was devoted to a case study presentation. At this point participants had the opportunity to discuss a case study brought by a school and to develop strategies and an action plan to support the pupil, staff and the parents/carers, if appropriate, using a formal problem solving technique. This forms Part Three of the book.

As a result of the workshop sessions participants were able to build up a training manual and handbook of practical resources to use in their own schools. This book is based on that training manual and handbook.

It is possible to use each section of the book separately or to use the entire book to set up an action research programme in school to test the efficacy of peer support systems for teachers.

Peer support systems in the context of whole-school behaviour policies

Peer support for teachers has to be seen within the context of a whole-school behaviour policy. Peer support systems will be an effective forum for teachers to use only if they form part of the overall structure and processes in place to manage pupil behaviour. Effective behaviour management can be seen as a three-tiered approach (see Figure 1). At level 1 there are the values and beliefs that the whole school community has agreed. This might be a general statement about expectations, positive relationships and the celebration of success and achievement. At this level there would also be agreement about matters such as curriculum delivery, marking and assessment and levels of supervision around the school and during the lunch break.

Running parallel to what has been agreed at level 1 is what happens in the classroom at level 2. Flexibility at level 2 is important given differences in teaching styles and the nature of the lesson being taught; however, all teachers should ensure that pupils are aware of the rules, consequences and rewards that operate in the classroom. Teachers should also take note, for example, of classroom organisation, the availability of equipment, and appropriate, expected behaviour for different activities, and the impact all of these may have on pupil behaviour. What is agreed at this level must be reconciled with the overall ethos and expectations agreed by the school community at level 1.

No matter how effective a school is at promoting and supporting positive behaviour at levels 1 and 2 it is still necessary to have a third level in which systems and procedures are in place to support individual pupils experiencing difficulties. Most schools will have sophisticated systems for developing individual education plans through the Code of Practice. There may also be systems and procedures in place for accessing the support of external agencies

MANAGING BEHAVIOUR IN A WHOLE-SCHOOL CONTEXT

Whole-School Issues

Desired behaviours	Promoting positive behaviour	Discouraging poor behaviour	Other factors
What are the values our school seeks to promote? What are our expectations?	Have we agreed to implement a specific model of behaviour management, e.g. Assertive Discipline? How do we positively recognise good behaviour? What whole-school reward systems do we have? What criteria are there for rewarding positive behaviour? Is the curriculum broad, balanced and suitably differentiated? Are there extra-curricular activities? How do we involve parents/carers?	How do we monitor poor behaviour? Are our assessment and recording procedures effective? Are the whole-school sanctions fair, consistent and effective? What criteria are there for the use of sanctions? Do they follow a least to most intrusive intervention? Is the purpose of our sanctions understood by all? Do we involve parents/carers quickly enough?	Are our levels of supervision outside the classroom effective? Does the organisation of the school day minimise poor behaviour? How is this policy cross-referenced with other relevant school policies? Is our staff support network sufficiently structured to be effective?

Classroom Management Issues

Desired behaviours	Promoting positive behaviour	Discouraging poor behaviour	Other factors
Are there class rules which have been developed with the pupils? Are they clearly displayed? Do they highlight the behaviours we want (rather than what we do not want)?	How do we positively recognise those pupils who follow instructions and rules? Is our reward system consistent with the whole-school approach? Do we focus on the positive rather than the negative? Have we informed parents/carers?	Are there consequences which have been agreed with the pupils? Are they clearly displayed? Is this consistent with the whole-school approach? Are we consistent in our application of consequences? Have we informed parents/carers?	Do we pay sufficient attention to: • organisation of materials and equipment • seating arrangements • teaching the appropriate routines for all the activities going on in the classroom, e.g group work, class discussion, etc.

Issues Relating to Individual Pupil Behaviour

Desired behaviours	Promoting positive behaviour	Discouraging poor behaviour	Other factors
What is the purpose of the IEP? Have targets been arrived at through systematic assessment and recording processes? Are the targets SMART? Has the IEP been communicated to all relevant members of staff? Were the pupils and parents involved in developing the IEP? Is the pupil given the opportunity to discuss progress?	Does the IEP have success criteria built in to monitor progress? Are there identified rewards which reflect the pupil's interests? Are the parents/carers involved in the reward system? Has this been communicated to everyone?	Are there clear consequences for not reaching/maintaining targets? Have these been discussed with the pupil and parents/carers? Have these been communicated to everyone?	What other support systems are in place to support this pupil? Are outside agencies involved and communicated with? Is there someone in school with responsibility to manage this pupil's behaviour plan? Have review dates been set up in advance? Has this pupil been the subject of a peer support meeting?

Figure 1 Adapted from *Developing a Behaviour Policy and Putting it into Practice,* Leeds Positive Behaviour Group, Galvin and Costa (1992) Leeds City Council

such as educational psychologists and behaviour support teams. Developing formal peer support networks for teachers at this level provides schools with additional support within their whole-school approach to behaviour management that acknowledges the skills, expertise and professional judgement of those teachers who know the pupil best.

Peer support systems and LEA support services

The initial rationale for developing peer support networks in schools was in part to offer schools a way of working together as a team that was not dependent on outside support services such as the school psychological service and behaviour support service. The reasons for this were twofold. Firstly, we were hearing more and more from schools, that support from educational psychologists and outreach teachers was limited because of the heavy caseload they had. Secondly, in looking with schools at their behaviour policies it became apparent that enshrined in some school behaviour policies was the notion that somewhere outside of the school was a magic solution to the challenging behaviour of some pupils. It was important, therefore, to encourage schools to take responsibility for finding solutions to challenging behaviour through mutual support, and as a consequence initiate a more dynamic relationship with external support services.

Once schools have decided to set up formal peer support systems, the LEA needs to make decisions at policy level to establish how it can support schools in this process. This can be done in a number of ways. For example, the development of peer support systems can form a major part of the LEA's behaviour support plan, which should be proactive and preventative rather than reactive and interventionist. Within this there might be an expectation that support services would agree with schools to provide training for part of the workshop sessions or that outreach teachers and psychologists might occasionally be facilitators of peer support meetings. Training in the development of peer support networks could be part of an induction programme for new staff to schools as well as support staff working in an advisory capacity for the LEA.

Special schools and pupil referral units can be encouraged to move toward this model of working, particularly within their policies for reintegration. Special schools and pupil referral units might even become centres of excellence for this practice and promote the notion of teamwork in the management of emotional and behavioural difficulties both within the special and mainstream school phases. This could be achieved through their work on reintegrating pupils back into mainstream schools and the promotion of inclusive education. Similarly, the peer support model presented forms the basis for partnerships of schools to work together as pupils transfer from primary to secondary school or between schools in the same phase.

The development of peer support systems across an entire education authority affords LEAs the opportunity to provide and promote a systemic approach for managing pupil behaviour in schools, in which collaboration is complete rather than piecemeal.

This has further possibilities if peer support is then extended to include other agencies, for example the health service and social services, thus creating a genuinely collaborative inter-agency approach to supporting pupils and teachers in schools. Inevitably, this will have training implications for teachers and others for which the LEAwould need to take some responsibility. However, a coherent programme of training to promote the idea of developing peer support systems for teachers has the added advantage of ensuring that everyone involved in supporting pupils with challenging behaviour does so with one voice.

Peer support systems and schools as learning organisations

Effective and improving schools, standards and achievement are perennial issues concerning everyone in education. Research into what makes an effective school is well known and the work of Sammons *et al.* (1995) has had a profound effect on providing schools with a purposeful lead in making appropriate changes in order to raise levels of pupil achievement. MacGilchrist *et al.* (1997) have further synthesised this work and suggested that one of the 'core characteristics of an effective school is a school with staff who are willing to be learners and to participate in a staff development programme'. These authors have also contended that 'continuous learning – for everyone – is central to the notion of the intelligent school'. It has already been suggested that an important part of the peer support meeting is the professional development element of the workshop. Certainly, teachers at peer support meetings are keen to develop action plans for the management of individual pupils as presented in the case studies. However, it is important for the overall health of the school that this support is coupled with an opportunity for staff to reflect on and challenge current practice in the management of pupils with emotional and behavioural difficulties. It is also a time to introduce to members of a peer support meeting new practices, and ultimately to combine this with an opportunity to develop a course that can be accredited by a local higher education institution. Ongoing peer support meetings enable senior managers, teachers, and other support staff to consider a range of educational topics concerning school improvement within the context of live issues relating to individual pupil behaviour. It is to be hoped that within this context teachers will feel empowered to request training that will enhance their practice in a variety of areas. Michael Fullan has written that 'educational change depends on what teachers do and think. It's as simple and as complex as that' (1991). The underlying rationale for peer support is that it adds to the total experience of what teachers do and think and so contributes to positive change within the learning environment of all pupils.

Peer support systems and inclusive education

Inclusive education means many things to many people and is often dependent on the particular special educational need. The basic premise of this book is that pupils with emotional and behavioural difficulties have special educational needs as 'simple and as complex' as other special educational needs. The government has stated that 'the education of children with special needs is a key challenge for the nation. It is vital to the creation of a fully inclusive society ...' (DfEE 1998). Furthermore one of the key themes set out in the Green Paper was to promote 'the inclusion of children with SEN within mainstream schooling wherever possible...' (DfEE 1997). These are sentiments with which the majority of educationalists agree. However, what teachers, support services and LEA officers find most taxing is how best to achieve this aim. Initially setting targets for inclusion looks to be a way forward and yet this cannot be the complete answer to the conundrum. Target setting can only be successful if it is accompanied by strategies for achieving targets, including detailed success criteria to monitor and celebrate achievement on each and every step of the way toward inclusive education. If teachers are expected to encourage, support and include pupils with emotional and behavioural difficulties then it is crucial for teachers to feel encouraged and supported themselves. For the majority of pupils, teachers and other adults in school are the only professionals with whom they have contact on a daily basis, and therefore teachers are in a unique position to offer pupils new learning experiences in order to meet their special educational needs. Hanko (1985) has suggested that these opportunities may be lost if teachers are not encouraged to deepen their knowledge and understanding through appropriate in-service training. More recently educationalists who promote inclusive education have suggested that schools should become research communities where staff development is as important as the emotional, social and academic development of its pupils. Developing peer support systems for teachers in school gives focus to teachers' learning and supports them as they work toward more inclusive education for pupils with emotional and behavioural difficulties. Through formal peer support networks, teachers can learn collaboratively to ensure that the inclusion of pupils with emotional and behavioural d i fficulties is successful. One of the suggestions made in the government paper *Meeting Special Educational Needs. A programme of action* (DfEE 1998) is that there should be a 'programme of peer consultancy...through which schools ...can obtain support and advice from their peers'. The purpose of the work carried out in Oxfordshire schools and described in this book offers one model of 'peer consultancy' that supports teachers in providing an inclusive and effective education for pupils with emotional and behavioural difficulties.

Part One

Conducting a needs analysis in school and identifying and assessing pupil behaviour

He who can interpret what has been seen is a greater prophet than he who has simply seen it.

(St Augustine De Genesi ad Litteram)

This part of the book deals with the value of carrying out a needs analysis and behaviour audit of a school's requirements in relation to behaviour management. There are a variety of questionnaire s, checklists and observation schedules for senior managers, teaching staff and learning support assistants to use in assessing not only the needs of pupils with emotional and behavioural difficulties but also the needs of staff in relation to managing behaviour in school. Analysis of the data will provide the basic knowledge and understanding of how best to support colleagues in the workplace. Some of the data collected will be useful in informing the content of the professional development elements of the peer support meetings.

Developing peer support systems for teachers offers staff in schools a new and dynamic way of working in teams to manage pupil behaviour. It is therefore important that schools undertake a needs analysis and audit of their total environment beforehand. This can take the form of questionnaires to staff and pupils, an audit of behaviour management in the classroom and around the school, and classroom observations. This will provide a useful baseline in order to carry out an evaluation of the peer support process in addition to meeting the needs of individual pupils and should be undertaken before the workshops on developing peer support systems begin and can be repeated after an agreed time.

Carrying out a needs analysis in school has three main purposes. Firstly, it is important to be aware of and assess the school's current p rocesses and strategies for managing pupil behaviour. This establishes what the school is doing in relation to behaviour management and whether there are consistent and agreed structures and systems for managing behaviour.As a result of work undertaken in Oxfordshire schools over several years we were aware that of all the matters associated with special educational needs the management of behaviour often caused the most stress among

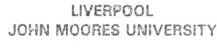

teachers in schools. It often had a damaging effect on teachers' self-esteem and their confidence in being able to manage the behaviour of pupils with diverse emotional and behavioural needs. One questionnaire (see Form 1, p.10) examines which areas of behaviour management cause teachers most stress and whether this could be altered by the development of a regular, structured peer support system. It is also important to establish the relationship between schools and outside support agencies and how this is to be used in order to maximise teamwork within a structured peer support system. Secondly, it is essential to develop a process for assessing the success or otherwise of a structured peer support system, and to do this some kind of baseline needs to be established. Included in this baseline there should be an agreement about performance indicators to judge whether peer support for teachers is an effective way of dealing with behaviour difficulties in school. Finally, it is important to have some kind of assessment of what schools might find useful as content for the professional development element of the peer support meeting, and to know in which areas of behaviour management schools might need more support. This knowledge is as important for support services as it is for the school itself. Running parallel to this is the need to stress that emotional and behavioural difficulties are not necessarily something that can be dealt with by a constant focus on individual pupils and their perceived deficits. The purpose of the process of developing peer support systems for teachers is to begin to establish a culture whereby schools are willing to undertake a thorough analysis not only of pupil behaviour but also of their perceptions of managing behaviour. In order to do this schools have to be prepared to undertake an audit of what the school, as an institution, is doing to create an atmosphere that promotes and values positive behaviour and teamwork (see Form 2, pages 14–20). (The Pupil Reinforcement Survey (Form 3, pages 21–22) affords schools useful, additional information from the pupil's perspective.)

In the Introduction a strong link is made between the development of peer support systems for teachers and schools as learning organisations, and the contribution this can make to increase the effectiveness of schools in terms of levels of achievement. In this section, therefore, the means are provided for schools to undertake their own action research projects to assess whether the development of formal, structured peer support systems might contribute to a more effective school.

'Being able to observe pupil behaviour is an important skill for anyone working in schools to develop.' (East Devon Behaviour Support Team 1993). The activity of observing pupil behaviour in the classroom or around the school must be seen as a supportive activity and is designed to be part of the process of supporting teachers and other colleagues in the workplace. It is important to stress that observing pupil behaviour in the classroom is a non-judgemental activity, which, nonetheless, is designed to challenge preconceived notions about the management of behaviour. Whilst anecdotal information can be valuable, objective observations to record specific information and behaviours depersonalises the activity and helps to create a culture in which support for staff is more than an empathetic response to dealing with problem behaviours. Observing behaviour in the classroom can provide a school with information about pupils on- and off-task behaviours, about teachers' rates of praising and the contribution this makes to establish a positive classroom climate. It can provide schools with quite specific information about behaviour in the classroom and around school as well as forming part of the school's overall behaviour audit. Monitoring individual pupil behaviour is very important for those pupils who are likely to become the subject of a peer support meeting. While it is sometimes necessary and valuable 'to tell a story' about an individual pupil, it is much more effective to be able to provide objective information which will guide the peer support meeting into developing an effective and purposeful action plan to support both pupil and staff through a difficult time.

Objectivity

When a pupil is causing concern in terms of their behaviour it is easy to assume that they are misbehaving all the time, particularly if the teacher is feeling under stress and pressure. At these times teachers often fall into the trap of saying that the pupil's behaviour also covers the entire range of inappropriate behaviours. Furthermore, it is often difficult to appreciate that sometimes the pupil is not misbehaving but actually engaged in purposeful learning. Observing pupil behaviour enables the teacher to stand back and examine what is really happening without being caught up in the situation. It offers a time for reflection, and the opportunity to share with colleagues what occurred and how the difficulties may be overcome.

Clarification

Careful observations will enable teachers to clarify in some detail the most important aspects of a pupil's behaviour and help us to find answers to some questions. For example, is it possible to describe what triggers a certain kind of behaviour? Is there a pattern to some behaviours, and do they occur at certain times in the school day? Are some behaviours reinforced by the behaviour of other pupils or by the reaction of adults in the room? Collection and analysis of this information will enable teachers to discuss with colleagues at a peer support meeting what is happening and how best to develop an action plan with appropriate strategies that will encourage the pupil to change his or her behaviour. It is also a useful tool for opening a dialogue with both pupils and parents/carers in a non-judgemental way, and can be used to involve parents/carers in working in partnership with the school to further support pupils at home and at school. It is helpful, therefore, to involve pupils in the process by getting them to complete the Pupil Reinforcement Survey (See Form 3, pages 21–22).

Why observe pupil behaviour?

Form 1

STRESS IN TEACHING

Stress Inventory for Teachers

How to complete the inventory. Please read the following instructions carefully.

The events listed in the inventory that follows have been included because some teachers say they feel stress when the events occur, or immediately afterwards. This survey is designed to find out which of these events occurred during your school day and how much stress, if any, you felt as a result.

The inventory should be completed on three separate days for the same week. (Photocopy sufficient as appropriate)

Please complete this front sheet carefully and on the days agreed by the staff team regardless of how unusual the day has been. If you are absent on any of the specified days please complete on an alternative day the following week. Please ensure that the new date is clearly marked.

In rating the amount of stress for each event you should consider the intensity and duration of your feeling and, if appropriate, how frequently the event occurred. For example, you might decide to give a rating of 'Very stressful'to the event 'The weather made the pupils restless', because although the stress was minor it lasted throughout the day. You might also rate the event 'A pupil was rude/hostile', as 'very stressful' because although the encounter was brief it left you feeling upset for a long time.

Remember it is your initial reaction that is important. Do not dwell on each question. Please do not complete the questionnaire with colleagues. The events listed are deliberately wide-ranging and in no particular order. This questionnaire is anonymous.

Please add any clarifying comments at the end of each page, if appropriate.

Thank you for completing this questionnaire. The results will be given to the whole school staff as soon as they have been collated.

BEFORE YOU START

Which day is this inventory for? Please fill in the date and circle the appropriate number below. Continue to circle the appropriate number on the inventory.

Day One	Date:	1	
Day Two	Date:	2	
Day Three	Date:	3	

Form 1 *continued*

	Did not occur	Not stressful	Slightly stressful	Moderately stressful	Very stressful
My teaching equipment was inadequate	1	2	3	4	5
My planning was unsatisfactory	1	2	3	4	5
There was at least one behaviour issue to deal with in the class	1	2	3	4	5
Some pupils did not do as they were told straight away	1	2	3	4	5
I was concerned about the safety of the pupils	1	2	3	4	5
The lesson did not begin well	1	2	3	4	5
There was insufficient time to do as I had planned	1	2	3	4	5
I had to do a playground duty	1	2	3	4	5
A pupil refused to follow instructions	1	2	3	4	5
Pupils did not achieve what I wanted this lesson	1	2	3	4	5
A pupil was verbally abusive to me/other pupils	1	2	3	4	5
A pupil was physically threatening towards me/other pupils	1	2	3	4	5
A pupil deliberately defied me	1	2	3	4	5
I had to give too much time to one pupil	1	2	3	4	5
I had to cover a lesson for a colleague	1	2	3	4	5
It was difficult to give time to individual pupils	1	2	3	4	5
Pupils did not listen to instructions	1	2	3	4	5
A member of staff annoyed me	1	2	3	4	5
My lesson was interrupted by callers to the class	1	2	3	4	5

Form 1 *continued*

	Did not occur	Not stressful	Slightly stressful	Moderately stressful	Very stressful
I was not consulted on a decision that affected me	1	2	3	4	5
I did not teach this lesson well	1	2	3	4	5
I felt another member of staff was observing me critically	1	2	3	4	5
Too many things happened at once and I found it hard to cope	1	2	3	4	5
Some pupils did not seem motivated by this lesson	1	2	3	4	5
It was difficult to bring this lesson to a satisfactory conclusion	1	2	3	4	5
An inspector was present during this lesson	1	2	3	4	5
The weather made the pupils restless	1	2	3	4	5
It was the first lesson after a wet break time	1	2	3	4	5
Apupil was rude/hostile	1	2	3	4	5
I had to collect/check money for lunch/trip/ school fund	1	2	3	4	5
Pupils were very noisy this lesson	1	2	3	4	5
Apupil(s) was late for this lesson	1	2	3	4	5
I disagreed with another member of staff	1	2	3	4	5
Ameeting after school was on my mind	1	2	3	4	5
There was a lot of clearing up to do at he end of this lesson	1	2	3	4	5
There was a significant group in this class that were difficult to manage	1	2	3	4	5
The pupils found this lesson difficult to understand	1	2	3	4	5

	Did not occur	Not stressful	Slightly stressful	Moderately stressful	Very stressful
I was unhappy about a recent SMT decision	1	2	3	4	5
I was thinking about the paperwork I needed to complete	1	2	3	4	5
I was thinking about the next parents evening	1	2	3	4	5
I was involved in an after-school activity	1	2	3	4	5

Other (please specify and rate)

	1	2	3	4	5
	1	2	3	4	5
	1	2	3	4	5

The day as a whole

	Not stressful	Slightly stressful	Moderately stressful	Very stressful
I found today as a whole was	1	2	3	4
For me this day of the week is usually	1	2	3	4

The state of my health today was ...(circle the appropriate rating)

Better than usual	Same as usual	Worse than usual	Much worse than usual
1	2	3	4

How many days have you been absent because of your own illness over the last term? Do not include school holidays if this is this start of a new term or half term.

_____days

Today for me was:

Fairly typical   1

Not typical   2

If not typical please say why (e.g. class outing, special activity)

_____

_____

_____

Reprinted with permission from D. Galloway, based on an original by J. Pratt, Victoria University of Wellington/NZ Educational Institute.

Form 2

MANAGING BEHAVIOUR IN THE CLASSROOM AND AROUND THE SCHOOL

This questionnaire is designed to provide an overview of the kinds of behaviours teachers have to deal with in the classroom and around the school. It asks teachers to reflect on their teaching during the week immediately prior to completing the various checklists.

The questionnaire also asks teachers to reflect on the effectiveness of the rewards and sanctions they have used, and on the strategies they would prioritise for dealing with difficult behaviour.

The kinds of behaviours detailed are deliberately wide-ranging and are in no particular order. Please add any behaviour you have experienced or strategies, rewards and sanctions you have used if they are not listed. There is space at the bottom of each page for you to add additional comments you think are appropriate.

The questionnaire is anonymous. Do not spend too long considering each question.

Please read the instructions carefully at the top of each page before completing the questionnaire and add any clarifying comments at the bottom of each page if appropriate.

Thank you very much for taking the time to complete this questionnaire. All staff will be told of the results as soon as they have been collated.

Form 2 *continued*

What type of pupil behaviour have you had to deal with during the course of your classroom teaching last week? You may tick as many boxes as is appropriate.

Type of behaviour	At least once during the week	At least daily
Talking out of turn (e.g. by making remarks, calling out, chattering)		
Calculated idleness or work avoidance (e.g. by delaying start to work, not having books or equipment)		
Hindering other pupils (e.g. by distracting them from work)		
Not being punctual (e.g. by being late for lessons, school)		
Making unnecessary, non-verbal noises (e.g. by scraping chairs, banging objects)		
Persistently infringing school and/or class rules		
Getting out of seat without permission		
Verbal abuse toward other pupils (e.g. by using offensive and/or insulting language)		
General rowdiness, horseplay or mucking about		
Cheeky and/or impertinent remarks or responses		
Physical aggression towards other pupils (e.g. by pushing, punching, striking or kicking)		
Verbal abuse toward you or other staff members in the class (e.g. by using offensive, threatening, insulting or insolent remarks)		
Damage to property (e.g. by breaking objects, damaging furniture and/or the building)		
Damage to own work or work of others		
Physical aggression to you or other staff members in the class		

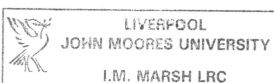

15

Form 2 *continued*

Please indicate the type of behaviours you have found most difficult to deal with *(that is, those behaviours you have experienced during your last week of teaching)*. If you have not had to deal with any of the behaviours listed during your last week of teaching leave the box blank. Please use the following scale:

1 = most difficult

2 = very difficult

3 = difficult

4 = not too difficult

5 = easy to manage

Type of behaviour	1	2	3	4	5
Talking out of turn					
Calculated idleness or work avoidance					
Hindering other pupils					
Not being punctual					
Making unnecessary, non-verbal noises					
Persistently infringing school and/or class rules					
Getting out of seat without permission					
Verbal abuse toward other pupils					
General rowdiness, horseplay or mucking about					
Cheeky and/or impertinent remarks or responses					
Physical aggression towards other pupils					
Verbal abuse towards you or other staff members in the class					
Damage to property					
Damage to own work or work of others					
Physical aggression to you or other staff members in the class					
Other (*please specify*)					

What types of pupil behaviour have you encountered and dealt with during the course of your duties around the school last week. You may tick as many boxes as is appropriate.

Type of behaviour	At least once during the week	At least daily
Lack of concern for others		
Unruliness while waiting to enter classrooms or queuing for lunch		
Running in the corridors		
General rowdiness, horseplay or mucking about		
Persistently infringing school rules		
Verbal abuse towards other pupils		
Loitering in prohibited areas		
Cheeky or impertinent remarks made to you or other staff members		
Physical aggression towards other pupils		
Leaving school premises without permission		
Damage to property		
Damage to work displayed around the school		
Verbal abuse towards you or other staff members		
Physical aggression towards you or other staff members		

Form 2 *continued*

Please indicate the type of behaviours you have found most difficult to deal with *(that is, those behaviours you have experienced in your duties around the school last week).* If you have not had to deal with any of the behaviours listed during your duties around the school last week leave the box blank. Please use the following scale:

1 = most difficult

2 = very difficult

3 = difficult

4 = not too difficult

5 = easy to manage

Type of behaviour	1	2	3	4	5
Talking out of turn					
Lack of concern for others					
Unruliness while waiting to enter classrooms or queuing for lunch					
Running in the corridors					
General rowdiness, horseplay or mucking about					
Persistently infringing school rules					
Verbal abuse towards other pupils					
Loitering in prohibited areas					
Cheeky or impertinent remarks made to you or other staff members					
Physical aggression towards other pupils					
Leaving school premises without permission					
Damage to property					
Damage to work displayed around the school					
Verbal abuse towards you or other staff members					
Physical aggression towards you or other staff members					
Other (*please specify*)					

Please indicate by ticking the relevant boxes the strategies and sanctions you have used to deal with difficulties in the classroom during the last week and their perceived effectiveness.

Type of strategy or sanction	Used		Effectiveness	
	At least once	More than once	Most effective	Least effective
Reasoning with pupil(s) in the classroom setting				
Warning and rule reminder				
Application of hierarchy of consequences				
Tactically ignoring minor infringements				
Follow-up discussions with pupil(s) outside the classroom setting				
Keeping pupil(s) in at break/lunchtime				
After school detentions				
In-class time out				
Time out of classroom				
Removing privileges				
Sending pupils direct to SMT				
Putting pupil(s) on report system				
Focusing on the positive behaviour of other pupils				
Using planned reward system				
Using a classroom discipline plan developed and agreed with pupils				
Other *(please specify)*				

Form 2 *continued*

Please indicate what you consider to be a priority for dealing with difficult behaviour in school at present. Use a scale of 1 to 5 where 1 is the top priority. Please grade each suggestion by putting a tick in the appropriate box.

Type of behaviour	1	2	3	4	5
Establishing smaller classes					
Tougher sanctions for certain forms of indiscipline					
More opportunities for counselling for pupils with the most challenging behaviour					
Increasing links with parents					
Adoption of whole-school behaviour management model (e.g. Assertive Discipline)					
Rolling programme of in-service training delivered by support agencies					
Network of peer support for staff in school					
Network of peer support for staff with other schools					
Adoption of pupil mentoring programme					
Developing closer links with the wider community					
'Buddy' system for staff using outside support agencies					
'Buddy' system for staff using own resources					
Developing a range of curriculum initiatives to support pupils with emotional and behavioural difficulties					
Spend time examining different teaching and learning styles and their effectiveness					
Change the ethos of the school					
Create more opportunities for team teaching					
Create more opportunities to observe colleagues in the classroom with feedback.					
Enhanced role for a member of staff to act as key worker/mentor for most vulnerable pupils					
Other *(please specify)*					

Form 3

PUPIL REINFORCEMENT SURVEY

The Pupil Reinforcement Survey should be completed by _____ pupils in Year _____.

The following questionnaire is designed to provide an overview of the kinds of rewards pupils seem to value most and the types of sanctions that might be most effective.

Staff who administer the questionnaire should try to ensure that pupils attempt all the questions but they do not need to complete all the spaces provided. On the other hand they can write more if they would like. Staff can help the pupils with reading, understanding and scribing but *should not* help them to answer the questions.

Staff may wish to read the whole questionnaire through with the pupils before they complete it.

A. Please tick three of the following. The school subjects I like *best* are:

English	❑ Maths	❑ Science	❑
R.E.	❑ Information Technology	❑ History	❑
Geography	❑ French	❑ Art	❑
Design & Technology	❑ P.E./Games	❑ Other *(please name)*	

_____

_____

_____

B. Please tick three of the following. The school subjects I like *least* are:

English	❑ Maths	❑ Science	❑
R.E.	❑ Information Technology	❑ History	❑
Geography	❑ French	❑ Art	❑
Design & Technology	❑ P.E./Games	❑ Other *(please name)*	

_____

_____

_____

C. The three things I like most to do at school are:

1. _____

2. _____

3. _____

Form 3 *continued*

D. If I had 30 minutes free time each day at school I would most like to:

1. _____

2. _____

3. _____

E. At break and lunch time I most like to:

1. _____

2. _____

3. _____

F. If I am asked to help in class I most like to:

1. _____

2. _____

3. _____

G. At home the three things I like to do most are:

1. _____

2. _____

3. _____

H. If I have done something wrong at school the sanction I like least is:

1. _____

2. _____

3. _____

I. If I have done something wrong at home I like it least if:

1. _____

2. _____

3. _____

J. If I have done a particularly good piece of work or have behaved particularly well I like it best if:

1. _____

2. _____

3. _____

Thank you for taking the time to complete this questionnaire. We will tell you the results when they have all been collated.

Providing a baseline

If the purpose of a peer support meeting is to encourage a team approach in developing procedures, systems and strategies to further support pupils with emotional and behavioural difficulties, there needs to be a clear understanding about what it is teachers are seeking to change. It is therefore important that accurate, dated records are kept that enable the teacher to set targets, review progress and note success. It also means that teachers are in a good position to set new targets and share this information with colleagues who have not taught the pupil before or been part of the peer support meeting.

Finally, schools that have developed a culture of teamwork through objective observations of behaviour in the classroom are in a position to extend the notion of teamwork to colleagues in other institutions including pupil referral units and special schools. It provides an effective model of working for those concerned with the transition of pupils with emotional and behavioural difficulties from the primary to the secondary phase. Equally it is a useful model to employ for those concerned with the reintegration of pupils from either pupil referral units or special schools back into mainstream education. If schools are able to carry out observations of this kind as part of good practice in the management of pupils with emotional and behavioural difficulties, it immediately challenges the support services to reassess their way of working with schools. Traditionally educational psychologists and teachers with behaviour support teams have seen observation as part of their function. If this becomes part of the school ethos and culture then support services are challenged to develop more dynamic, innovative and effective ways of working with their colleagues in school.

How to observe pupils in the classroom or around the school

There are many ways of observing behaviour in the classroom or around the school. The main thing to decide is precisely what needs to be observed and then choose a method that will yield the necessary results.

Event recording

Behaviours that have a clear beginning and end can be recorded using this method. Event recording (see Form 4) notes the number of times a specific behaviour occurs over a specific period of time. It is best to record this in numerical form or as tally marks. Event recording can be used to observe for example how many times: the pupil calls out during a lesson; the pupil gets out of his or her seat; is late for lessons; or arrives ill-equipped for a lesson. Using this method of observation several times over a period of several days can be helpful in demonstrating patterns of pupil behaviour. This method of observation can be used to note rates of teacher praise (see Form 5), or how often the teacher interacts either positively or negatively with boys or girls in the classroom (see Form 6). Each of these observations can be used to assess how positive the atmosphere is in the classroom. This method of observation is usually not useful in recording behaviours that occur for extended periods of time.

Form 4

EVENT RECORDING

Choose a behaviour that has a clearly defined beginning and end e.g. calling out. (Substitute your own on the photocopiable sheet). Record with tally marks the number of times the pupil uses this behaviour over a specific period of time. This could be done all day every day for a week or at specific times during the day over a longer period.

Name of Pupil: _____   Class: _____

Date: _____

Behaviour	Activity – e.g. group work, individual work or whole-class teaching/discussion	Before break	After break	After lunch
Calling out				
Wandering around the room				
Arriving late for lesson				
Ill-equipped for lesson				

RECORDING RATES OF TEACHER PRAISE/APPROVAL

Observation key:

+	In this column write 'T' for task related positive feedback (i.e. to do with work). Or write 'B' for behaviour related positives.
Sp. (Specific)	Put a tick in this box if it is very clear who is receiving the positive feedback (i.e. a group or individual is named or it is a private, personal word). This can also be used to record the gender of those receiving the positive feedback.
Des. (Descriptive)	Tick here if the behaviour or work is described as part of the positive feedback, e.g. 'Thank you for sitting down immediately', 'Well done, that is much better presentation of your work', 'Thank you for raising your hand'.

Use the boxes below to record the positive feedback

Date and Time of Observation: _____

Class/Group: _____

Activity/Lesson: _____

+	Sp.	Des.	+	Sp.	Des.	+	Sp.	Des.

Form 6

RECORDING NEGATIVE FEEDBACK

Use the boxes below to record rates of negative feedback using a simple tally chart. Photocopy extra quantity of forms as required.

Date and time of observation: _____

Group/Class: _____

Activity/ Lesson:_____

Task set or instruction given *(any type)*	Negative feedback to individual	Negative feedback to group	Negative feedback to whole class

On and off task recording

This method of observation is helpful to use when pupils have difficulty in concentrating, or a tendency to hinder other pupils' learning. The pupil is observed for a fixed period of time during a lesson and a record is kept as to whether the behaviour observed indicates that the pupil is either on or off task. On task behaviour can be defined as following the teacher's instructions and off task behaviour is doing anything else. The recording sheet can be even more sophisticated by using a key to describe off task behaviours more precisely. This method of observation can be used in two ways (see Form 7, p.29):

- The pupil is observed for 5 minutes every 15–20 minutes during a lesson. A check is kept of the total number of times the pupil remains on task during the 5 minutes of observation.
- The pupil is observed at short regular intervals over a 20 minute period. A note is made as to whether the pupil is on or off task at the moment of observation. It is important to keep a close eye on a watch (a second hand is vital) to record only the behaviour observed at the time and to avoid the temptation to record those behaviours that occur outside the observation time. It should be decided in advance how long is going to be spent doing the observation overall.

ABC recording

This is a detailed written record of pupil behaviour (see Form 8, p.30). It is a method whereby the observer can record what happens immediately before the described behaviour and what happens immediately after the described behaviour (A = antecedent, B = behaviour, C = consequence). This can be very revealing and is a useful tool for enlisting the support of the whole class or small groups of pupils to help an individual pupil change his or her behaviour. Similarly it enables teachers to develop a better understanding about how their behaviour or classroom organisation may contribute to pupils behaving inappropriately.

Analysing pupil behaviour

As well as observing pupil behaviour it is also a good idea to carry out a behaviour audit in order to understand what other external factors may be impacting on pupil behaviour (see Form 9, pages 31–32).

Each of these methods of observation will generate sufficient data to make a detailed assessment of behaviour in the classroom, which will enable staff, pupils and parents to come to a decision about what needs to be changed. Learning schools can use observations of behaviour and whole-school behaviour audits to inform their rolling programme of professional development to increase the effectiveness of their institutions. Observations such as these meet the requirements of the Code of Practice and assist toward the development of individual education plans.

Analysing all the data can be a reassuring activity. It is often the case that pupils are observed to be on task far longer than had previously been judged. Careful analysis makes it far easier to highlight those behaviours that are repeated and need to be changed. Purposeful dialogue with pupils, parents and colleagues can be initiated on the basis of the observations, which clarify what might be contributing to some behaviour difficulties. Everyone is offered an opportunity to reflect on their behaviour and the consequences of their behaviour on others. Suddenly, it becomes easier to assess and analyse 'what makes it difficult for teachers to teach and pupils to learn' (Elton Report 1989).

The data can be analysed in a variety of ways and the results should be appropriately and accurately recorded. Graphs can be designed as well as tally sheets and frequency charts. The value of recording the data is that monitoring and evaluating the action plan can be carried out again after a period of time using the same observation sheets. This is sometimes best done when the action plan has been in place for at least a month and possibly six weeks. It can be so beneficial if everyone is able to see the results of both sets of observations in diagrammatic form. It is tangible evidence of progress being made and of the capacity to achieve change and improvement.

Based on an analysis of the data gathered, a peer support meeting is an effective forum in which an action plan can be developed to promote and support the agreed changes. It is a forum in which success criteria can be determined to keep everyone on the right path, as well as monitor progress. It is a forum in which all members of staff can receive maximum support in the management of change with least damage to their own self-esteem.

Form 7

TIME SAMPLING OBSERVATIONS

Pupil: _____**Date:**_____

Activity/Lesson:_____

Behaviour key:

On task/following directions	1
Talking (positive)	2
Interacting with peers (positive)	3
Interacting with adults (positive)	4
Talking out of turn	5
Making noises	6
Turning round	7
Out of seat (inappropriate)	8
Throwing things around	9
Hindering other pupils	10
Day dreaming	11
Other (specify)	12

Time   **Behaviours**

	1 minute	2 minutes	3 minutes	4 minutes
15 seconds				
30 seconds				
45 seconds				
15 seconds				
30 seconds				
45 seconds				
15 seconds				
30 seconds				
45 seconds				
15 seconds				
30 seconds				
45 seconds				
15 seconds				
30 seconds				
45 seconds				
15 seconds				
30 seconds				
45 seconds				

Form 8

ABC RECORDING

Pupil: _____ **Date:** _____

Activity/Lesson: _____

Behaviour Objectively describe the behaviour. Be specific.	Antecedents What happened immediately prior to the unwanted behaviour?	Consequences What happened immediately after the behaviour occurred?
1.		
2.		
3.		
4.		

BEHAVIOUR AUDIT

The purpose of this behaviour audit is to assist schools in exploring what is working well, where behaviour difficulties are occurring and where change is likely to be most beneficial. The results of this behaviour audit might be used to inform the professional development elements of the peer support meeting, and some of these areas are covered in Part Two of this book. Please use the following scale.

1 = In place and working well. No need for further development.
2 = In place but inconsistently applied in school.
3 = In place but not working well. Need for review and further development.
4 = Not in place.

Level 1: Whole-School Behaviour Policy

	1	2	3	4
School has an effective behaviour policy				
The behaviour policy is understood by the whole school community				
Rules are communicated frequently to the whole school community				
Staff know and use the range of rewards available to the pupils				
Staff know and use the range of sanctions that can be used				
Staff use mainly preventative strategies for behaviour management				
Pupils understand the purpose of the behaviour policy				
There are clear links between this policy and other policies in school				
Staff are clear about roles and responsibilities				
Staff feel confident to acknowledge difficulties				
Staff know where to go for help and support and do so				
There is a rolling programme of INSET relating to behaviour				
Support services are used efficiently and effectively				
Parents are consulted at all levels of behaviour management				
Parents are routinely told of pupils' good behaviour				
Governors are involved in policy development and implementation				
Routines for movement around the school are clear				
Rules for the lunchtime and break time are understood by everyone				
Rules for the lunchtime and break time are consistently applied				
Supervision outside the classrooms is monitored and effective				
'Hot spots' are identified and problems overcome				
Suitable activities/equipment available for all break times				
There are effective systems for conflict resolution				
Other *(specify)*				

Form 9 *continued*

Level 2: Behaviour Management in the Classroom

	1	2	3	4
Equipment is easily accessible				
Furniture arranged to best effect				
Lighting, temperature, ventilation appropriate				
Materials well labelled				
Ease of movement in the room				
Pupils' belongings easily stored				
Pupils grouped appropriately for different tasks				
Chalk/white board visible to all pupils				
Wall displays reflect current work				
Teacher arrives at lesson on time				
Instructions are clear				
Purpose of the lesson is explained				
Good behaviour is noticed and recognised				
Small achievements are acknowledged				
Adults in the room act as good role models for desired behaviour				
Materials and equipment are prepared				
Lessons are well prepared				
Adults are well prepared to deal with poor behaviour				
Curriculum delivery is varied				
Curriculum is appropriately differentiated				
Pupils come to lessons with correct equipment				
Pupils are encouraged to work collaboratively				
Support in the classroom is used effectively				
Rules are few in number and displayed				
Rules are developed with the pupils				
Rules are frequently referred to and used to reinforce good behaviour				
Rules are positively phrased as far as possible				
Rewards are consistently and fairly used				
Rewards are valued by the pupils				
Rewards link with whole-school reward system				
Consequences/sanctions are understood by pupils				
Consequences/sanctions are consistently and fairly applied				
Consequences/sanctions are hierarchical				
Rewards and sanctions are understood by parents/carers				
There are routines for entering and leaving the classroom				
Signal for getting attention of the class is understood				
There is established routine for getting teacher's attention				
There are routines for distribution of materials and equipment				
Pupils know when and how to move around the room				
Pupils know the routines for tidying up at the end of lesson/activity				
Other *(specify)*				

Part Two

Peer support systems and professional development

Communication skills in the classroom

This chapter deals with communication skills and focuses on supporting teachers to develop effective listening skills and to learn questioning and negotiating techniques. It will provide a foundation for one-to-one work with pupils who are causing particular concern. This chapter will also provide a range of exercises and activities that participants in the peer support group can practise with each other before using them in the classroom. Overall, the aim of this chapter is to encourage teachers to develop a more assertive approach to behaviour management.

Developing good interpersonal skills is important for all teachers. Understanding and having the ability to draw on a range of counselling techniques will enhance interpersonal communication and help to build trusting relationships between teacher and pupil, which are fundamental to the healthy emotional development of all pupils. There are many theoretical models to draw on in the development of counselling skills. The model underpinning this work is the Adlerian model, to which there are four phases:

(i) The initial phase entails establishing an empathetic relationship in which the pupil feels understood and accepted.
(ii) The second phase requires an exploration and assessment of the pupil's beliefs, feelings, motives and goals.
(iii) The third phase involves interpretation and insight in order to help the pupil perceive themselves and the situation in a different light.
(iv) The final phase requires reorientation and action, to enable the pupil to consider alternative attitudes, beliefs and action, while encouraging a commitment to change.

Establishing an empathetic relationship

When a person is able to feel and communicate genuine acceptance of another, he possesses a capacity for being a powerful helping agent for the other ...It is one of those simple but beautiful paradoxes of life: when a person feels that he is truly accepted by another as he is then he is freed to move from there and begin to think about how he wants to change, how he wants to grow, how he can become different, how he can become more of what he is capable of being. (Gordon 1970)

In establishing an empathetic relationship it is important to be aware of verbal and non-verbal cues which can be a barrier to communication. Research suggests that certain kinds of communication have a therapeutic or healthy effect on people. They can make us feel better, encourage us to talk, help us to express our feelings, foster feelings of worth or self-esteem, reduce threat or fear and thereby facilitate growth and constructive change. Other kinds of talk are 'non-therapeutic' or destructive. These messages tend to make people feel judged or guilty: they restrict the expression of honest feelings, make us feel threatened, foster feelings of unworthiness and low self-esteem, block growth and constructive change by making us defend more strongly the way we are (Rogers 1969, Gordon 1970).

Through his work with parents and teachers, Gordon (1970) developed the use of a 'language of acceptance' which he suggests is the most essential factor in establishing an empathetic relationship. In order to demonstrate this quality, the development and practise of specific skills is required. These are 'active listening', 'reflective responding' and 'open questioning'. In furthering the practise of effective communication skills that facilitate the development of positive relationships between adults and children, Gordon identified several categories of verbal response, all of which he described as having a destructive effect on relationships. These are:

- ordering, directing, commanding
- warning, admonishing, threatening
- exhorting, moralising, preaching
- advising, giving solutions or suggestions
- lecturing, teaching giving logical arguments
- judging, criticising, disagreeing, blaming
- praising, agreeing
- name calling, ridiculing, shaming
- interpreting, analysing, diagnosing
- reassuring, sympathising, consoling, supporting
- probing, questioning, interrogating
- withdrawing, distracting, humouring, diverting.

Rather than using any of this repertoire, Gordon advocated the technique of 'active listening'. This requires that the listener does not send a message of his own by way of response during an interaction – for example, an evaluation, opinion, advice, logical argument, analysis or question. Instead it involves the use of responses that do not communicate any of the listener's own judgements, ideas or feelings but invite the speaker to speak. For example:
'I see . . .Oh. . .Really. . .Ah yes. . .Go on. . .Right. . .Tell me more. . .OK. . .'
The use of active listening enables pupils to say more of what they feel, to go deeper and develop their thoughts further. It helps pupils to find out exactly what they are feeling. After they express their feelings, the feelings often seem to disappear as if by magic. Active

listening fosters this kind of catharsis. In addition, it also influences the pupil to be more willing to listen to the ideas and thoughts of others. Thus active listening is one of the most effective ways of helping a pupil to become more self-directing, self-responsible and independent and also to be more socially responsible and aware.

Exercise 1

Active listening

Divide group members into pairs and ask each to identify themselves as either A or B. Ask the As to think of a subject that they would like to discuss with their partner. They will need to sustain a conversation for one or two minutes. While the As are thinking of the focus of their conversations take the Bs to one side. Tell them that they will listen to their partner's conversation for two periods of about one minute each time. In the first period they must adopt a posture which communicates a lack of interest in what is being said to them. In order to do this they may choose from the following range:

- Sit with legs crossed and look away from the speaker from time to time.
- Keep arms and legs crossed and maintain expressionless face, yawning intermittently.
- Appear restless and fidgety and look away from the speaker to remove imaginary specks of dust or fluff from their clothes.
- Fold hands behind their head, stretch out their legs and cross their ankles.
- Do not maintain eye contact but look up at the ceiling.

Stress the fact that this part will be hard to do and may feel very uncomfortable. On a given signal to mark the end of this first period they may then utilise all the strategies they know to encourage their partner to talk. This can include non-verbal as well as verbal messages and should give opportunity to practise the range of active listening techniques.

Discuss the exercise as a whole group giving both As and Bs an opportunity to describe their thoughts and feelings as well as the potential use of this activity with pupils in the classroom.

'Reflective responding' takes the concept of active listening one step further and involves the use of mirroring techniques to reflect back to the pupil some recognition of an understanding of what they are thinking and feeling. In reflecting back content, paraphrasing is used with lead-ins such as:

'It seems that. . .You think it's. . .You find it. . .
It seems as though. . .Could it be that. . .'

In reflecting feelings the same technique is used but with the listener now receptive to the feelings behind the words, and response is thus focused on clarifying and articulating these:

'It seems that you are feeling ... Could it be that you feel ... Maybe you feel. . .'

Exploration and assessment

Exercise 2a

Reflective responding (content)

In pairs choose to be A or B. A talks for two minutes while B listens either non-verbally or with Uh-mm responses. B then recalls through paraphrasing what A has said with no additional comments or questions. Discuss the experience for a few minutes then change roles and repeat.

Exercise 2b

Reflective responding (feelings)

In pairs choose to be A or B. A talks for two to three minutes about a strong emotional memory from childhood. B reflects back feelings by tentatively suggesting 'You felt . . .'. Change roles and repeat this process. Discuss as a whole group your thoughts and feelings about this exercise.

Interpretation and insight

The correct use of 'questioning techniques' can also enhance the quality of the relationship and enable the pupil to be self-reflective and insightful in regard to themselves and others. A general rule of thumb is that 'Why' questions should be avoided. 'Open questions' and questions with 'I messages' (Gordon 1970, Millar 1991) will keep the communication going and encourage the pupil to explore the problem further while allowing them to retain ownership and a sense of independence and responsibility. Open questions can be used to encourage the elaboration of a point:

'Could you say a little more about that?'

They can be used to encourage the expression of thoughts and feelings:

'What does this mean to you? I'm wondering how you feel about that?'

They can also be used to encourage more detail:

'Could you say what it is about . . .that upsets you? When you say. . .what exactly do you mean?

'I messages' are a very useful technique to employ in communicating effectively with others. 'I messages' require the sender to state their own feelings clearly in a communication and avoid the use of blame, which 'you messages' convey. A simple formula to use in sending 'I messages' is:

"When . . .I feel. . .because. . .".

For example:

'When there is so much noise I am unable to concentrate on the work I am doing, because I find it too distracting. I would like you to work more quietly, please.'

as opposed to:

'You are far too noisy. That's enough!'

'I messages' are a far more effective communication for the teacher to use, and are therefore more likely to be heard and responded to by the class. The key to developing this style of communication is that the messages conveyed are non-judgemental. Thus 'I messages' offer the means by which to convey a feeling without blaming the receiver of the communication.

Exercise 3

·'I messages'

In pairs A asks B a barrage of questions for a minute or two about what the other person is wearing or doing. A remembers the questions and turns them into 'I messages'. For example, 'Where do you get your hair done?' might become 'I've been admiring your hair for some time and wondered where you go to have it cut?' In a whole group discussion compare the two styles.

Once the pupil has gained insight into their concerns they can begin to consider alternative actions and attitudes. At this phase they need to be able to establish realistic goals and will therefore need help to explore and understand the problem, define the goal and choose an alternative course of action.

Reorientation and action

Exercise 4

Problem solving

- Divide the group into pairs and ask each pair to work on a particular problem. At this stage it may be appropriate for the group facilitator to have cards with a variety of scenarios written out for the group to use. Problems might include lateness for lessons, failure to hand in homework or inability to work appropriately during literacy hour. Alternatively, scenarios illustrating everyday dilemmas could be used.
- Each partner in the pair could role play the scenario.
- Each pair should discuss the problem so that they agree on what the main issues are. Active listening skills can be used in this discussion.
- Each pair should then decide on the task to be achieved. Open questioning will facilitate this part of the exercise.
- Once each pair has defined their goal they should explore all the alternatives that might help them achieve their goal. Brainstorming is an effective way to gain as many ideas as possible in a short space of time. Be prepared to consider questions such as 'What do you think might happen if...?' 'How might you feel if...?' 'Have you considered...?' All the alternatives should be thoroughly discussed.
- The next step is for each pair to evaluate all the possible solutions. Some may have to be discarded because they are impractical. Each pair should focus on summarising the ideas and evaluating their potential.
- Having chosen a possible solution each pair might want to discuss issues around the question 'What do you think will happen if you do this?'
- Once each pair is committed to a particular solution they should devise an action plan to implement their solution. This might include a contract. There should also be some agreement about how the action plan is to be monitored and evaluated.

(Adapted from: Counselling Skills Set A, Millar 1991)

Such a hasty exploration of the rudiments of effective communication skills will not turn the teacher into a fully trained counsellor, nor is it designed to do so. The purpose of these exercises is to give teachers and other staff confidence in developing a deeper level of communication when having to support groups of pupils or individual pupils experiencing behaviour problems in school. It will also provide pupils with an effective model of interpersonal skills on which to build their own relationships. Their use will thereby enhance the learning environment within the classroom. Finally, it is important to emphasise the need for teachers to practise these skills and techniques before using them with pupils and the peer support meeting is a useful forum in which to do this.

Developing a classroom discipline plan

This chapter will demonstrate the importance of a classroom discipline plan and will provide the opportunity for members of peer support groups to experience how they might develop a classroom discipline plan with their pupils. The chapter will focus on the three main elements that are necessary for the creation of an effective classroom discipline plan. It will also capitalise on the main themes of the previous chapter and explore how teachers can use a language of discipline to ensure that pupils can be encouraged to follow the discipline plan by making right choices.

Charles (1996) suggested that it is only in the last 50 years that teachers have given serious consideration to using a classroom discipline plan as a positive means to encourage pupils into positive behaviour rather than reacting to inappropriate behaviour. However, it would be fair to say that the majority of teachers acknowledge the importance of developing a classroom discipline plan with their pupils at the start of the school year, which is regularly reviewed and revised as the year progresses. Nonetheless, this is worth revisiting as part of the professional development element of peer support meetings. Many educators have devised a variety of theories for understanding pupil behaviour, but they all agree that clear, firm guidelines for establishing boundaries relating to what is acceptable, and consistently applied consequences for what is unacceptable, are paramount in supporting all pupils in their learning.

A classroom discipline plan consists of three parts; each part is dependent on the other and each part is of equal importance. If a classroom discipline plan is to be effective, all three parts have to be in place. The whole purpose of a classroom discipline plan is to make it 'easier for teachers to teach and pupils to learn' (Elton Report 1989). In making it 'easier for teachers to teach and pupils to learn', a classroom discipline plan creates a positive classroom climate in which pupils can be encouraged to think about their rights and their responsibilities within a learning environment.

Rules

A classroom discipline plan consists of rules, rewards and consequences. Rules should be clear, positively stated and enforceable. They should be few in number and wherever possible inclusive language should be used. Rules should be developed with the pupils and displayed in the classroom. Some educators, for example, Canter and Canter (1992), have argued that as far as possible rules should only refer to observable behaviours. Thus, rules that articulate notions of respect are vague and open to individual interpretation. On the other hand, rules that articulate specific behaviours are not open to interpretation (e.g. *'keep your hands and feet to yourself'*. Although different classrooms may develop different rules, often relating to the lesson being taught, it is important that the class rules can be reconciled with the overall ethos of the school. Some schools have developed a set of rules that are applicable throughout the school day and in any area of the school building; for example, rules relating to punctuality, equipment and polite language. Class teachers are then in a position to develop further rules that relate to the variety of activities pupils are expected to undertake in any given lesson. It is important that in developing rules with pupils in the classroom they are not seen to be arbitrary but an expression of the rights and responsibilities of the teacher and the learner.

Exercise 1

Why have class rules?

(Facilitators should adapt this exercise depending on the numbers taking part)

- A group of about 8 participants is necessary. Participants not taking part should act as observers.
- Ask about 8 people to join you in a circle.
- Remind any remaining participants that they are to act as observers.
- Explain that you will use a stem sentence, which begins: 'My name is . . .[add your own name]. I am going to Alaska and I am taking a . . .' [add an object that matches the first initial of your name].
- So the sentence may go 'My name is Lynne and I am going to Alaska and I am taking a lamb with me.'
- The next person is invited to repeat the sentences adding their own name and object. If they both begin with the same initial the group facilitator responds with 'You can' but if not then with 'You can't'.
- Give clues if the game is in danger of dragging on and invite the observers to help out if they can.
- The purpose of this game is to get the participants to experience feelings relating to knowing and not knowing the rules. Participants will also experience other feelings as 'the penny drops!' (Bond 1990).
- When the activity is finished discuss their feelings about this exercise, as a whole group.
- Relate this to how pupils might feel if the class rules have not been developed and clearly explained to them.

Rewards or positive ways to recognise pupils when they do well are an important part of any class discipline plan. In the peer support work undertaken in Oxfordshire schools teachers all agreed that their schools did have detailed reward systems in place. However, they also agreed that they were usually inconsistently applied and as a result not rated very highly by the pupils. It is, therefore, useful to revisit this element of the classroom discipline plan during a peer support meeting. However, discussions around rewarding pupils for positive behaviour can be sensitive and some teachers argue convincingly that pupils should not be rewarded for doing as asked and as expected. Nonetheless, in line with a whole-school approach to managing behaviour, it should be possible to reach an agreement whereby members of the whole school community understand the importance of valuing and recognising the achievements of others in that community. In doing this it is possible to create a sense of belonging to a group which elicits appropriate behaviour both from pupils and adults.

Rewards can be given in a variety of ways. The most obvious is the non-verbal and verbal recognition that can be given for learning and behaviour. In the pupil reinforcement survey completed by pupils in primary and secondary schools in Oxfordshire, the majority of pupils stated that if they had completed a good piece of work or had behaved particularly well they just 'wanted to be told'. Some pupils said, in the same survey, that although they valued the reward systems in place, they were rarely used. Non-verbal and verbal rewards have the advantage of being immediate, but the adult giving the reward should ensure that it relates to the task or the activity and not the person. These kinds of rewards can also be given privately, which suits the needs of some pupils.

It is possible to offer rewards that convey status (Lund, R. 1996). This might include certificates, trophies and badges and can be celebrated in public if the pupil finds this acceptable. Sometimes rewards that convey status can be awarded to the whole class, particularly in relation to behaviour and attendance. This helps in emphasising to the pupils their personal responsibility for the well-being and overall achievement of the whole class or group. Finally, rewards can take the form of particular treats – for example, extra break time, privileges and time to undertake a favourite activity. This would be subject to the age of the pupils, size of the school and the overall school organisation. At most of the peer support meetings in Oxfordshire, teachers admitted how often parents/carers were contacted when things were not going well, and how infrequently when things were going well. Informing parents/carers of the good news was recognised as a potent reward.

Canter and Canter (1992) emphasised the need for teachers to take the opportunity to praise every pupil they teach at least once every day. When this was presented to teachers in the peer support meetings it was met with some degree of incredulity. It was felt that it was an impossible task. However, as a group, participants were encouraged to develop and rehearse a script that would enable them to do this. Those teachers who tried this out in the classroom reported back on its success and the improved atmosphere in the classroom overall.

Consequences The final part of a classroom discipline plan concerns the consequences or sanctions it is agreed should be in place for those who choose not to follow the agreed rules. As with the rules, the consequences need to be reconciled with the agreed ethos and values of the school. Generally speaking, schools in Oxfordshire have found that a set of consequences that are hierarchical and ensure that pupils are able to maintain their self-respect have been most effective as long as they are consistently applied. Participants at peer support meetings noted that the use of consequences was most powerful when they were offered as a choice in which the pupil was given the chance to behave more appropriately. As with the use of praise and encouragement members of the peer support meeting were offered the opportunity to work on developing a script that could be practised with each other before trying it out in the classroom. One of the advantages of having a class discipline plan with a preplanned script for its implementation in the classroom is that it eases the pressure on teachers and resists the temptation of having an ad hoc response and inconsistent approach to behaviour management.

The ultimate purpose of a classroom discipline plan is to support pupils into appropriate behaviours and to get them to understand the effects of their behaviour on others and to encourage the development of self-discipline.

Exercise 2

Developing a classroom discipline plan

- As a whole group, brainstorm all the rights everyone has in the classroom.
- Work with the whole group to categorise each of the rights into appropriate groups, e.g. rights relating to learning, movement, communication, safety, respect, problem solving (Rogers 1992).
- Divide the peer support meeting into smaller groups, if appropriate.
- Ask the groups to use the following pro forma to develop a class discipline plan or review their discipline plans currently in place.
- Ensure that equal time is given to all three parts of the discipline plan.
- Allow all members of the peer support meeting time to share their discussions with each other.

Classroom Discipline Plan

Rules *(few in number, relating to observable behaviours and positively stated)*

Rewards *(encourage positive self-esteem, recognition of achievement in learning and behaviour, emphasise wanted behaviours, provide positive feedback)*

Consequences *(realistic, hierarchical and respectful)*

Exercise 3

Rehearsing a script to use a discipline plan effectively.

- Divide the group into groups of 3 or 4.
- Get each group to devise a script that starts with an instruction for the class related to a work activity. If necessary the course facilitator can give each group an opening sentence.
- Ask the group to continue making up a script using the class discipline plan to offer rule reminders and the application of rewards and consequences.
- Get them to take turns in using the script on each other.
- Bring the smaller groups back as one whole group to discuss how they felt this worked and how it might work in the classroom.
- This can also be tried as a whole-group exercise.

An example of such a script to help with this exercise could be as follows:

Teacher: *I'd like you to get your textbooks out please and open them at page 15 ready to look at the Causes of the First World War.* **(Rule: Follow instructions the first time of asking.)**

Well done Amanda and Brian, I can see you're ready to start work. **(Reward: Verbal praise and encouragement.)**

Bill, I asked the class to get their books out. I need to remind you about our rule relating to following instructions and ask you again to get out your textbook. **(Consequence: Rule reminder and first warning.)**

Bill, this is the third time you have chosen not to get out your text book. If you are going to continue to choose not to do as you have been asked you will have to come back to class for five minutes at lunch time. **(Consequence: Using the agreed hierarchy.)**

Bill: It's not fair. Carole keeps talking to me and disturbing me.

Teacher: Perhaps she does but I am asking you to get your text book out ready to start work. So, if you choose not to follow this instruction then you will be choosing to come back to class for five minutes at lunch time.

(Adapted from Canter and Canter 1992, Rogers 1994)

The pupil should then be given the chance to follow the instruction without the teacher standing right beside him or her. In other words the teacher should assume that the pupil would now do as requested. The pupil should be immediately rewarded when he or she does comply with the request. If the pupil continues not to do as asked the teacher should carry on with the agreed consequences.

The facilitator of the peer support meeting might want to encourage the group to use this script as a basis for making up their own to practise. Teachers in Oxfordshire who have done this work have agreed that developing a language of discipline to implement their classroom discipline plan has contributed to a more positive atmosphere in the classroom. Equally, it has been a powerful tool for managing off task behaviour that detracts from teaching and learning time.

Understanding behaviour and dealing with difficulty

This chapter will examine one model of behaviour management that teachers taking part in the peer support work in Oxfordshire found particularly useful. On the basis of this chapter schools may choose to look at other models of behaviour management. Alternatively, schools may introduce the one outlined in this chapter as a further means of supporting pupils with emotional and behavioural difficulties by offering teachers a process by which they can begin to understand the purpose of some behaviours. Discussions that arise from this chapter should help the peer support group to focus on the importance of consistency throughout the school when dealing with behaviour issues.

> We should recognise that the misbehaving child is only trying to find his place: he is acting on the faulty logic that his behaviour will give him the social acceptance he desires.
>
> (Dreikurs and Cassel, 1972)

Rudolf Dreikurs was an American child psychiatrist who has made an enormous contribution to understanding children's behaviour. His work has particular relevance for understanding behaviour in the classroom, and working with pupils directly to try to reach amicable solutions to challenging behaviour. Dreikurs' ideas are based on Adlerian psychology and one basic premise that 'Man is a social being and his main desire is to belong.' (Dreikurs 1972). Pupils' behaviour, therefore, has a purpose, which is to belong and find a place within the group, whether that group is the class group, the group in the playground or the family group. Dreikurs has further argued that when pupils behave appropriately and are recognised for that, they are less likely to misbehave. On the other hand, when pupils misbehave it indicates that they have a mistaken belief about how they can belong. It follows that if the teacher, other adults or other pupils reinforce the misbehaviour, pupils may then believe that they have found their place and the misbehaviour may be repeated. Dreikurs believed that teachers have a responsibility to use the class group to help understand the misbehaviour of some pupils and so help them to belong in more appropriate ways.

Dreikurs observed four goals of misbehaviour (Figure 2, page 49) and suggested that once teachers are able to understand the significance of the goals of misbehaviour they are then in a position to 'confront' their pupils with this. If teachers are successful in being able to do this they will get a 'recognition reflex' from the pupils. This shows that the pupils understand the purpose of their misbehaviour and teacher and pupil can then begin to work on alternative more appropriate behaviours. This process is dependent on teachers being 'psychologically sensitive' to the purpose of pupil behaviour.

Using this model of understanding behaviour is dependent on teachers using a process that starts with observing pupil behaviour in a systematic way and having some understanding about how such behaviour makes the adults in the classroom feel. It is necessary to have an understanding of the goals of misbehaviour and have the ability to talk about this with the pupil in a calm and non-judgemental way. The process ends with either individual pupil discussions or group discussions to support pupils in feeling as if they are able to belong through more acceptable behaviours.

Exercise 1

As a whole group brainstorm the kinds of qualities participants would like to nurture in the pupils they teach.

Record all the responses onto some flip chart paper.

The facilitator should have a pre-prepared flip chart or overhead transparency listing the following characteristics as described by Dreikurs (1972).

"A well adjusted normal child will display most of the following criteria:

S/he
• has a true sense of his/her own worth
• has a feeling of belonging
• has socially acceptable goals
• meets the needs of the situation
• thinks in terms of "we" rather than just "I"
• assumes responsibility
• is interested in others
• respects the rights of others
• cooperates with others
• encourages others
• is courageous
• is willing to share rather than being concerned with "how much can I get?"
• is honest
• puts forth genuine effort

The peer support group should be given the opportunity to discuss and compare their list with the Dreikurs list

The facilitator should take time to link this with the four goals of misbehaviour described below and how the work can be used to support pupils with emotional and behavioural difficulties.

THE FOUR GOALS OF MISBEHAVIOUR

	ATTENTION	POWER	REVENGE	WITHDRAWAL
PUPIL'S MISTAKEN BELIEF	I only belong to this group when I behave in a way that causes other pupils and adults to take more notice of me.	I am only able to belong to this group when I feel that I am in charge and that no-one can make me do anything if I do not want to.	I feel unloved and think that no-one cares about me. I can only belong to the group if I hurt others as much as I feel hurt.	I can only belong to this group if I can convince everyone not to expect anything from me.
THE TEACHER'S REACTION	Teachers may feel annoyed and irritated by this behaviour. They may try to coax he pupil into more positive behaviours or constantly remind them about their misbehaviour.	Teachers may feel angry and frustrated with pupils who behave in this way. Teachers who feel they have to win may enter into the power struggle. Or teachers might withdraw from the challenge and give in to inappropriate behaviours.	Teachers may feel equally hurt and discouraged. Some teachers might find it difficult to believe that pupils can behave in such a way. Others may find that they cannot like the pupil and begin to treat them unfairly.	Teachers confronted with this kind of behaviour may feel equally helpless. Sometimes teachers may withdraw themselves and allow the pupil to dictate the pace of learning. Some teachers may find it difficult to know how to encourage the pupil.
PUPIL'S RESPONSE TO THE TEACHER'S REACTION	The pupil's misbehaviour is reinforced and may continue. Or the pupil may use other inappropriate behaviours to gain attention.	Entering into the power struggle can escalate the problem and so intensify the power struggle. Passivity, in this case, may also encourage pupils to intensify their behaviour.	Pupils may feel that they are being unfairly treated thus creating feelings of hostility or humiliation. This may simply reinforce the pupils mistaken beliefs.	If passive pupils are met with passivity from their teachers (role models) they will find it more difficult to work hard and raise their levels of achievement.
SOME IDEAS FOR RE-DIRECTING MISBEHAVIOUR	Tactically ignore behaviour, where possible. Regular positive feedback whenever possible. Establish clear discipline plan.	Use an assertive language of discipline. Use "I" statements. Ensure pupil has responsibilities within the class/school. Allow the pupil to be a leader in some activities.	Use regular PSHE sessions to explore issues relating to co-operation, collaboration and relationships. Develop "peer support" for pupils	Focus on work that interests the pupil. Have success built into the tasks set. Celebrate achievement no matter how small. Send positive notes home.
ACCEPTABLE BEHAVIOUR: THE "WELL ADJUSTED CHILD"	The pupil contributes to activities and is helpful. The pupil volunteers for tasks but is not disappointed if not chosen.	The pupil is aware of the consequences and takes responsibility for his/her actions. The pupil is self-disciplined and is an effective leader.	The pupil works well in a collaborative group and is a good "team player." The pupil can maintain good relationships with most pupils even if they are not friends.	The pupil is courageous and is prepared to make mistakes. The pupil tries hard and is genuinely pleased with success and achievement. The pupil is concerned for others.

Figure 2 Adapted from: Dreikurs R. (1972) *Discipline Without Tears*

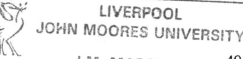

49

The four goals of misbehaviour

Attention seeking

These are the kinds of behaviours that Elton described as 'making it harder for teachers to teach and pupils to learn' (1989). They are often fairly low level but it is often the frequency and intensity of these behaviours that cause teachers most concern, and can include making noises, calling out and prodding other pupils. Pupils who are confident about their ability to belong will gain attention by contributing and volunteering for activities and tasks.

Pupil's Mistaken Belief: I am only able to belong to this group when I behave in a way that causes adults and other pupils to take more notice of me and continue to take notice of me.

The Teacher's Reaction: Teachers are often annoyed and irritated by the pupil's behaviour and may constantly remind the pupil about it, and try to coax him or her into more positive behaviours. Often teachers are successful in the short term but somehow the pupil then finds other inappropriate ways to gain attention. This often becomes annoying for other pupils in the class.

Power seeking

These behaviours often take attention-seeking behaviour one stage further. They can be behaviours that are associated with challenging authority, defiance, answering back and refusal to work. Sometimes teachers will describe pupils behaving in this way as stubborn, forgetful or lazy. Pupils who are able to find appropriate ways to belong are able to take responsibility for their actions and are able to demonstrate self-control and self-discipline.

Pupil's Mistaken Belief: I am only able to feel as if I belong when I feel that I am in charge and that no-one can make me do anything if I do not want to.

The Teacher's Reaction: Teachers usually feel angry and frustrated with pupils who behave in this way. This is often accompanied by a determination to win on the part of the teacher, which can escalate the conflict still further and intensify the power struggle. On other occasions teachers may feel threatened and defeated by the behaviour and tend to react more passively, thus giving in to the inappropriate behaviour.

Revenge

Pupils who seek revenge are usually deeply discouraged and will resort to behaviours like lying, stealing or verbal abuse in order to try and find their place. These pupils are often able to exploit the vulnerability of others and seem oblivious to the harm and hurt they may be doing. Sometimes these pupils are so discouraged that they may kick and hit out at other pupils also. Bullying is often associated with pupils who are trying to belong through revengeful behaviour. Sometimes the behaviours may be so extreme that a school will want to get extra support from outside agencies. Pupils who are able to belong using more appropriate behaviour recognise and understand the value and meaning of cooperation. These pupils are able to develop and maintain positive relationships and appreciate the concept of trust.

Pupil's Mistaken Belief: I feel unloved and think that no-one cares about me. I can only belong if I hurt others as much as I feel hurt. I am certain that no-one in this group likes me.

The Teacher's Reaction: Teachers often feel equally hurt and discouraged. Sometimes teachers might express incredulity that a pupil could inflict such pain on them or other pupils. At other times teachers may begin to feel that they cannot like the pupil who is causing the problems in the classroom. This can then lead teachers to ignore the carefully constructed class discipline plans and they may use more arbitrary sanctions that are inconsistently applied. The effect is often to create either feelings of hostility or humiliation, thus reinforcing the original inappropriate behaviours.

Withdrawal

Some pupils who have tried attention-seeking behaviour to achieve a feeling of belonging but without success may resort to behaviours in which they withdraw from any challenges with which they are confronted. This can be in relation to both their learning and their interaction with others. Sometimes these pupils will set themselves unrealistically high standards and then destroy their work when they feel they have failed. These pupils have little self-esteem and prefer not to try rather than try and not succeed. Such pupils are likely to be underachieving. Pupils who have high self-esteem have the courage to make mistakes and learn from them. They know that they can belong by participating and avoiding conflict.

Pupil's Mistaken Belief: I can only belong to this group if I can convince everyone not to expect anything from me. I am unable to meet targets and respond to challenges. I feel unable to complete this work.

The Teacher's Reaction: Teachers will often react to this type of behaviour by feeling equally helpless. They find it difficult to know how best to encourage the pupil and move them on to make progress. Occasionally, faced with such a task, teachers may withdraw themselves and leave these pupils to dictate the pace of learning. When passivity meets with yet more passivity pupils will find it hard to show improvement, to raise their levels of achievement and to make progress both in terms of their learning and behaviour.

Once teachers feel confident about understanding the four mistaken goals and have recognised their own feelings about the behaviour, it is important to confront the pupil. The purpose of confronting the pupil is to encourage the pupil to understand the purpose behind their b e h a v i o u r. This should be done in a calm and friendly manner and teachers should avoid making judgements. It is important when having this discussion with the pupil that the focus is on the pupil's intentions and purpose and how this might be changed. Focusing on what has

Confronting pupils with their mistaken goals

happened generally achieves little. It is useful to have a pre p a red script with which to confront the pupil, and the following may be of some use:

- Begin with a brief, objective statement about the behaviour observed and the consequence of that behaviour.

Then ask the following questions in turn:
Could it be that

- *You wanted me and/or the group to take more notice of you in that lesson? (Attention)*
- *You wanted to prove to me that you are in control and that I cannot make you do anything? (Power)*
- *You wanted to show me and the rest of the class what it feels like to be disliked? (Revenge)*
- *You are so worried about not being able to do the work that it is easier to sit back and do nothing? (Withdrawal)*

Having posed these questions teachers should look for a 'recognition reflex' after each one. Each question should be asked even if the 'recognition reflex' is apparent after the first question. This might take a number of forms including avoiding eye contact, smirking, shuffling uneasily in the chair or turning away. Once pupils are able to understand the purpose of their behaviour discussions can begin as to how the goal of belonging can be achieved through more appropriate behaviours. It is helpful for teachers to redirect a pupil's behaviour by noting and pointing out how other pupils are able to achieve attention, power, and approval by more appropriate means. It is then useful to develop with the pupil a plan that can be used to monitor and evaluate behaviour.

Ideas for redirecting pupil behaviour using this model

Attention
- Tactically ignore behaviour, where possible.
- 'Catch them being good' and positively recognise with encouragement.

Power
- Be assertive rather than either aggressive or passive.
- Use "I" statements.
- Engage the pupil in tasks that offer responsibility.
- Give the pupil opportunities to be a leader in group activities.
- Ensure the pupil has chances to help others in particular tasks.

Revenge
- Use regular classroom activities like Circle Time to develop positive, trusting relationships.
- Ensure that groups understand what is meant by cooperative, collaborative group work.
- Set up formal peer support systems for pupils.

Withdrawal
- Focus work on the interests of the pupil, as far as possible.
- Plan activities with guaranteed success.
- Acknowledge (quietly) all achievements, no matter how small.
- Send positive notes home.

Teachers need to be patient and consistent if they decide to use this model. It is also important to remember that activities during lesson time, especially PHSE lessons, can be used to reinforce those characteristics necessary for encouraging a sense of belonging in all pupils. This work should be ongoing and not set up as a direct result of our individual pupil's misbehaviour.

Exercise 2

- Ask each member of the peer support group to think of a pupil they know well and write a short paragraph about this pupil's behaviour. This need not detail a specific incident but can be more generally descriptive. It should include a couple of sentences about how the teacher feels about the behaviour.
- In groups of three or four, get the teachers to share what they have written with each other.

Then ask them to consider the following questions:

- What did the various descriptions of behaviour say about each pupil's purpose?
- What was the teacher's reaction to the behaviour? Did the pupil stop behaving in this way or was the behaviour reinforced by this reaction?
- How can each pupil be supported into more appropriate behaviours to achieve their goal and a sense of belonging?
- Open this out to discussion by the whole group.

The facilitator of the peer support meeting should allow time for each group to share their discussions with the group as a whole.

Part Three

Presenting a case study and problem solving

This section of the book will take readers through the process of a case study presentation resulting in the development of a range of strategies to support an individual pupil with emotional and behavioural difficulties. There is guidance for writing a case study, some examples of problem-solving techniques and some suggestions about accessing specific activities for supporting pupils in the classroom.

> Social psychologists have long believed that there is no such thing as a creative person, only creative groups. It is certainly the case that the thinking of all of us is highly influenced by the thinking of those with whom we talk and interact on a daily basis. On most occasions it is possible to be part of a group process that encourages, supports and rewards our potential for creativity. The ideas of others spark our own. The theory of one group member may help to build a much more creative theory by touching all kinds of new ideas among the rest of the group. When controversy is encouraged and diversity sought and used, a group can emerge in untold amounts of creative problem solving. (Johnson and Johnson 1997)

The case study should be written and presented in a way that feels most comfortable to the presenter and peer support group. However, following these guidelines may serve as a useful aide-mémoire. They should be adapted as necessary to suit the presenter and the needs of the group. Each member of the peer support group should have a copy of the case study as well as other relevant documentation, if appropriate. Although members of the peer support group may be very familiar with the pupil, there are real benefits if the author of the case study reads it aloud to the group.

Background information (if relevant)
- Family
- Preschool
- Previous schools

Guidelines for the case study presentation

55

An accurate and factual description of the pupil's behaviour
- In the classroom
- At home
- In the playground
- On the school bus (if relevant)
- Interaction with peers
- Interaction with adults
- Around the school

Be sure to use data collected from observations as exemplars of behaviour.

Pupil's Self-Perception
- What do I like doing at school?
- What don't I like doing at school?
- What do I think I am good at?
- What do I find difficult?

Did this pupil complete the pupil reinforcement questionnaire?

Indicate strategies used so far and the degree of success
- Classroom strategies
- Whole-school strategies including individual education plans
- External agencies

If you could make one wish for this pupil what would it be?

Case studies should be about two sides of A4 paper and take about 5 to 10 minutes to read out. Other members of the peer support group should be offered the opportunity to ask questions in order to clarify particular issues. But remember that the peer support meeting should be solution focused and the group facilitator must ensure that participants do not dwell on the problems and difficulties.

Problem-solving approaches

Brainstorm

Brainstorming is a process that encourages group members to think divergently and create between them a vast array of ideas in a short space of time. The facilitator of the peer support meeting should ensure that everyone participates in this exercise no matter how impractical the suggestions may seem. Everyone in the group should be invited to take part.

The first part of the brainstorm exercise is designed to encourage quantity and not necessarily quality at this stage. Once the process of divergent thinking has taken place, the facilitator of the group is in a position to lead participants into more convergent thinking in order to develop an action plan to support the pupil causing concern.

Rules for brainstorming
- Agree to focus on one area of difficulty or concern.
- The group should accept all ideas without judgement or criticism.
- Even the wildest ideas should be accepted. At this stage practical considerations are not important.

- The facilitator should emphasise and encourage quantity rather than quality during this part of the exercise. The more ideas generated now, the more likely it is that the group will have a varied range of strategies from which to develop a coherent action plan.
- The facilitator of the peer support group should start to build on the creativity of the group by pooling ideas and beginning to give some coherence to the emerging thinking.
- Everyone should be given the opportunity to contribute in a supportive and non-judgemental atmosphere.

After the brainstorming, all ideas should be categorised and evaluated for their possible use and practical application. The whole group should devise an effective action plan to support the pupil causing concern, or the group can be broken down into smaller groups of about four or five to work on an action plan (see page 60). The peer support meeting should then agree to the action plan as a whole group. This entire activity can be carried out in smaller groups, each group working on a different problem, with ideas shared by the whole group at the end of the exercise.

The facilitator may wish to practise the brainstorming technique with the peer support group first by getting them to brainstorm the uses of a paper-clip.

Force field analysis

Force field analysis is based on the assumption that changes in the present situation will occur only as the helpful and restraining forces are changed so that the level where they are balancing is altered ... Force field analysis is useful for two reasons. First it avoids the error of a single factor analysis of a problem ... Second, by helping to identify a number of problem related factors, it gives group members several points at which they may intervene in their attempts to produce change. (Johnson and Johnson 1997)

The use of force field analysis as a problem-solving strategy affords members of the peer support group the opportunity to look at all the factors that may be influencing the behaviour of individual pupils. If staff have already undertaken observations in the classroom and a behaviour audit, the results of this may also contribute to the restraining and helping influences affecting the pupil's behaviour.

Having shared and discussed all the restraining and helping forces, the peer support group is in a position to explore and examine which forces they are most likely to be able to reduce or enhance. At this point it will be possible to work on an action plan that will support the pupil and encourage change. The action plan could involve changes in the school environment as well as innovative ways of involving parents/carers and the support services.

Guidelines for using force field analysis as a problem-solving technique

- After the case study presentation, the peer support group should work as one group or in smaller groups of about four or five.

- The problem or problems causing most concern should be agreed. While it is reasonable for groups to work on different areas of concern, the peer support group should agree to initiate only one action plan at a time, unless there is an obvious overlap.
- Having identified the area of concern the group should reframe this into how they would like the situation to be.
- Next make a list of all the helping and restraining forces that affect the situation as it currently exists. Helping forces could include the strengths and interests of the pupil as well as external factors that have a positive effect on the pupil's behaviour. Restraining forces might include those forces that militate against change. However, the peer support group should be honest and include those factors relating to, for example, the quality of teaching, the curriculum and other school factors that might be having a negative effect on the pupil's behaviour.
- Review the two lists and underline those forces that the group believes to be the most important now and that, working as a team, the school staff might be able to influence. Depending on the group discussion, there may be just one force that stands out, or more than one in both lists.
- Take two or three of the underlined restraining forces and two or three of the underlined helping forces. Brainstorm strategies that might hinder the restraining forces and enhance the helping forces.
- Each group will now have a list of actions and strategies that may be able to change the key forces affecting the behaviour of the pupil. Review this list and decide which look as if it might be possible to use as the basis for an action plan (see page 60).
- Share the action plan with the whole group.

Boomerang

Boomerang is a very interactive way of working together as a team to try to solve problems. Although members of the peer support group work in pairs or small groups, it is nonetheless a genuinely collaborative process and generates a very varied set of strategies from which to devise an appropriate action plan. The boomerang problem-solving technique has two main aims: firstly, 'to encourage team ownership of a problem or difficulty, and, secondly, to promote a creative approach to problem solving' (Brandes and Ginnis 1990). Over and above this, it is a fun way to problem-solve and work together as a team. This method of problem solving resembles a game of consequences.

Guidelines for using boomerang as a problem-solving technique
- After the case study presentation the whole group should be asked to work in pairs or smaller groups depending on numbers. This method of problem solving works best if there are at least three smaller groups.
- The group facilitator should have prepared in advance enough sets of plain paper stapled together for each group.

- Each group decides on the issue causing them most concern. Once this has been shared with the whole group (to avoid overlap), the problem is written on the top sheet of paper in one or two precise, objective sentences.
- Each group passes their 'problem' on to the neighbouring group who discuss the issue, and on the first blank page in their set of papers brainstorm strategies to help solve the problem.
- The facilitator should allow only 5 to 10 minutes for this. The work is folded so it cannot be seen and the paper passed on to the next group.
- The process is repeated until each group has its original problem returned.
- If there is time the group can spend a few moments brainstorming possible strategies for their own area of concern.
- Each group reads through all the suggested strategies in response to their situation and selects the most favoured.
- Each group then devises an action plan, which can be shared with the whole group (see page 60).

There are other problem-solving techniques, but schools in Oxfordshire who took part in the peer support training found the three above the most popular and effective.

Action Plan for Support Programme for Individual Pupil

Targets	Action	Resources	Time/Review dates
What do we want to achieve?	How will we achieve what we want? What success criteria will we use?	What do we need to achieve what we want, including staffing? Who will take responsibility for monitoring?	

The following case study was presented to a peer support group consisting of two representatives from six schools in Oxfordshire. The 12 members of staff were either SENCOs or heads of year from middle and upper schools. The case study was written before the course had been completed and is, therefore, not as detailed or as objective as might be expected. Once the case study had been presented the group used force field analysis to develop an action plan to further support the pupil. The peer support facilitator provided a range of practical strategies and resources for staff to use in school to implement the action plan and other strategies.

An example of a case study

Vikki

Background information

Vikki is 12 years old and in Year 7. She is the third of four girls. Her three sisters are pleasant, friendly and outgoing. She comes from a stable family with both parents in work. Her mother works in the school canteen. Vikki seems well provided for and is always well dressed and neatly presented.

Vikki's mother has been concerned about her daughter's behaviour since the age of four years. She talked to the Health Visitor who recommended a referral to an educational psychologist. After Vikki's mother discussed this recommendation with a neighbour she decided not to proceed with the referral. Apparently the neighbour had suggested that Vikki might be taken into care. Vikki had glowing reports from her first school as the following extract from her Year 3 report shows:

> She thoroughly deserves the excellent progress she has made in all areas this year. She is a lovely, helpful, happy and caring member of the class . . .I wish she wasn't moving.

Vikki then moved to a second first school for her final year before transfer to middle school. At the end of Year 4 a lack of enthusiasm was noted in most subject areas, although staff were keen to point out that she had ability. Teachers commented that Vikki sometimes brought playtime troubles into the classroom and this was having a detrimental effect on her achievement and progress.

Behaviour

At home Vikki takes delight in 'winding up' other members of the family, with the exception of her mother who says it does not work on her. Vikki can be sullen and argumentative. Her mother says that, for example, Vikki constantly makes comments whilst the family are watching television and occasionally members of the family become so irritated that they leave the room.

Vikki started middle school in September 1995. Vikki's teacher was a mature NQT who left before the end of that term. He had become aware of Vikki's aggressive behaviour, and had received three complaints from parents about Vikki punching and kicking other pupils as well as damaging some pupils' clothing. By the October half term some pupils in the class were afraid to go out

---

at break and lunch times. In class Vikki was loud and constantly answered the teacher back. Her teacher discussed her behaviour with her, but she appeared not to care. Detentions were used as a sanction but they had minimal effect. After the teacher had left, the class had a succession of supply teachers throughout the remainder of the school year. The whole class was generally unsettled at this time.

In Year 6 Vikki's relationship with her peers was causing some concern. Her parents were invited to school to discuss Vikki's behaviour. She was loud, disruptive and rude to staff and pupils alike. Her parents were supportive and agreed to support school sanctions that consisted mainly of detentions. There was little improvement and in the Spring term Vikki was moved into another class. This seemed to work and there was a marked improvement in Vikki's behaviour.

In Year 7 Vikki's class had a temporary teacher for half a term, and then a part-time form tutor. During this time that particular year group did not have a year head. The class as a whole was unsettled and Vikki was causing increasing concern as an instigator of classroom disruption. Vikki was also becoming increasingly confrontational and challenging, even in situations that seemed to be non-confrontational. Her manner toward other pupils was becoming very threatening both physically and non-physically. Vikki was manipulative and sometimes incited other pupils to misbehave. A series of meetings was arranged with Vikki's mother and Vikki was seen by the deputy head and placed on a target report.

One incident

All Year 7 pupils were invited to a talk given by a visiting speaker. Vikki's tutor group had to wait in another Year 7 classroom prior to their turn to listen to the speaker. Two girls, on returning to that classroom, realised that the birthday presents belonging to one of them were missing from their school bags. The teacher asked the class if anyone knew anything about this and Vikki immediately began sighing and 'huffing'. She leapt to her feet shouting, 'I knew you would all blame me. Search my bag for all I care.' Vikki then walked toward the teacher, emptying and throwing items from her bag across the room. A hairbrush narrowly missed the teacher's head. The two presents were in the bottom of Vikki's bag. Vikki insisted that the dolls belonged to her and then insisted that if we did not believe her we should talk to her mother.

Positive comments

Vikki is able and as a school we have tried to focus on her academic achievements. She enjoys sport and is a good team member with leadership qualities. Her mother says that Vikki is good with younger children and will often seek out their company. After incidents in which Vikki is involved she is always sorry and expresses remorse.

Pupil's self-perception
Vikki is content with her overall academic achievements although she feels less confident about mathematics. She enjoys reading, creative writing and sport most of all. Vikki says she enjoys working with and helping younger children. She sees the main problems in terms of her behaviour occurring at breaks and lesson changeover times. She says that it is at this time that she feels other pupils harass her.

Strategies
A number of strategies have been tried including:

- Detentions
- Meetings with parents
- Time with trusted member of staff
- Time out
- Target setting and report sheets
- Exclusion

None of the above strategies have been successful in the long term, although some have had short-term success.

The most successful strategy was the change of class in Year 6. Vikki is now in a class with a teacher who is genuinely fond of her and would like Vikki to remain in this class until she goes on to upper school. At the moment Vikki is also happy with this arrangement.

Vikki is now on Stage 2 of the Code of Practice and a referral to the educational psychologist is being made. The outreach support teacher is also being involved.

Wishes for Vikki

- To achieve her academic potential without adversely effecting the education of other pupils in the class.
- To be happy about herself in the hope that she feels less inclined to make others feel as miserable as she seems to feel.
- To smile.

Force field analysis
The following analysis of the case study and suggested strategies are based on the discussions the peer support group had after the presentation. In this case the group of 12 broke down into three separate groups and each group took one of the three wishes for Vikki to work on as their reframed area of concern.

Group 1: Achieving her academic potential
The group identified the following restraining forces that hindered progress for Vikki. These included:

- Negative interactions with some staff and pupils.
- Instability of teaching staff.
- Vikki's self-image.
- Vikki's place in the family and the family dynamics.

However, the group also identified the following positive forces. These included:

- Good relationships with certain members of staff.
- Good leadership qualities.
- Enjoyed working with and helping younger pupils.
- Did have a previous record of academic success and positive relationships.

This group's strategies to support Vikki consisted of the following ideas:

- Encouraging Vikki's reading and writing skills by designing and publishing books for younger pupils.
- Creating opportunities for Vikki to work as a sports leader with younger pupils. This could be extended to developing links with neighbouring first schools.
- Since Vikki had got onto a roller-coaster of negative criticism it was felt that she should be encouraged to use a diary/planner in which only positive comments would be recorded.

Group 2: To be happy about herself so she feels less inclined to make others feel miserable

- The second group discussed very similar restraining forces, although they concentrated much more on gender issues within the family and the family dynamics in particular.
- Vikki's apparent bullying behaviour toward other pupils was also a matter of concern.

This group thought the positive forces that could influence Vikki's behaviour included:

- Her academic potential.
- Her ability to recognise when she might get into trouble and her attempts to try to do something about it.
- Her loving and supportive family.

This group's strategies consisted of the following ideas:

- Ensure that Vikki is given some kind of responsibility commensurate with her interests, e.g. sports captain.
- Capitalise on Vikki's appreciation of public praise and remind teachers and other staff to 'catch her being good' and recognise it immediately.
- Set up a meeting with Vikki's parents and discuss with them the importance of encouraging and praising Vikki as often as possible, trying to avoid Vikki being made into the family scapegoat. Set up a series of meetings that are designed to offer the family ongoing support.

Group 3: To put a smile on her face

- The restraining force that this group focused on was their perception that Vikki gained some very positive feelings about her success in being able to manipulate others.

- The other restraining force was the possibility that Vikki was suffering with PMT.

The positive forces discussed by this group were the same as the other groups.

- The strategies discussed by this final group included some contact with the outreach teacher who might be able to involve Vikki in some role play in order to encourage her to reflect on her feelings and gain some insight into her behaviour.
- The group also discussed involving the health visitor to work with the parents on a nurturing programme.
- But as with both other groups, it was felt to be important to encourage all adults to be positive with Vikki and try to ignore her negative behaviour.

The next stage for the peer support group as a whole would be to select those strategies that looked to be most useful and practical and set them out as an action plan using the chart on page 60.

In this particular instance the group facilitator and the peer support members decided on the following course of action to be taken back into school.

- The group was aware that Vikki could perceive some of the strategies used so far as negative. It was agreed to find time to release a learning support assistant to shadow Vikki and observe her behaviour and the behaviour of others using some of the observation schedules in Part One of this book. It was also suggested that it might be helpful to undertake a behaviour audit. The expectation was that it would then be possible to obtain an objective picture of what was happening to Vikki as she moved from lesson to lesson and during free association time.
- To work with staff in school using the communication skills exercises in Part Two, Chapter 1, to support them in their day to day interaction with Vikki. To support Vikki's form tutor to use the exercises to encourage Vikki to gain some insight into her behaviour and the consequences of her behaviour and then to help her to consider some alternatives.
- To work with all staff to develop a language of discipline during lesson times as discussed in Part Two, Chapter 2, to maintain consistency of approach from lesson to lesson and around the school.
- To explore Vikki's mistaken goals of behaviour as described in Part Two, Chapter 3. Use this information to challenge Vikki about her behaviour and work out some mutually acceptable strategies for redirecting her inappropriate behaviour.

The group also discussed other areas of concern and the facilitator was able to provide a range of practical strategies to support teachers in gaining some understanding of Vikki's behaviour. It also offered teachers a variety of activities that could be undertaken by the whole class or as small group work to support Vikki into more appropriate behaviours and relationships. Some of these exercises might form the basis of ongoing lessons in Personal, Social and Health Education or in work on citizenship.

The following list and accompanying resources provides an overview of some of the strategies that were discussed:

- Family constellation and the influence on an individual of his or her place in the family (Dinkmeyer *et al.* 1987, Millar 1991).
- Examining personality type and using this to build stronger personal relationships (Murphy 1992).
- Activities and exercises to encourage cooperation and collaborative group work (Curry and Bromfield 1994).
- Activities and exercises to explore issues relating to gender. (Curry and Bromfield 1994).
- Worksheets and group activities relating to developing positive attitudes and enhancing self-esteem (Bernard 1996).

Finally, it is useful to point out those elements of the peer support meeting that all course participants found most helpful. There was a unanimous feeling that the act of writing a detailed case study to present formally to a group of colleagues helped to focus the mind on the real issues of concern and to put the challenging behaviours into perspective. Some participants liked the formal structure of the meeting and the fact that it was solution focused, leaving less time to concentrate on the problems and difficulties; moaning was kept to a minimum! All participants were relieved to find that, although each pupil is unique, it was easy to share problems, note the similarities and gain a sense of belonging to a supportive group keen to share skills and expertise. A corollary of this is that all participants were reaffirmed in their own confidence and ability to support pupils with emotional and behavioural difficulties.

In conclusion it should be stressed that facilitators of peer support meetings ought to encourage group members not to opt always for larger than life solutions that might be seen as the answer to all prayers. Usually they do not exist. Often it is the obvious small changes that have the biggest impact and offer the maximum support. For example, changing a pupil's tutor group, moving a pupil into a different set or arranging to have a short daily telephone conversation with a parent/carer can make all the difference to a pupil's behaviour and ultimately to their capacity to benefit from their learning environment.

'Tiny differences in input could quickly become overwhelming differences in output' (Gleiche 1987).

'Change comes from small initiatives which work, initiatives which imitated, become the fashion. We cannot wait for great visions from great people, for they are in short supply at the end of history. It is up to us to light our own small fires in the darkness' (Handy 1995).

It has not been possible in this book to give more than a flavour of the work that was carried out with schools in Oxfordshire. It is a condensed version of some very intense peer support meetings carried out over a six-week period (as can be seen from the appendix on page 68), which included a variety of activities and exercises to encourage experiential learning. A genuine bond was created between all the participants and in each case the groups continued to meet on a regular basis. As a result of this, one group decided to set up a partnership literacy project in order to support pupils with poor literacy skills across the partnership of schools. In another case staff continued to meet to discuss the support of pupils causing concern. Other groups recognised the importance of setting aside time to work in this way and built it into their school development plan.

It has not been possible to describe in this book the enormous range of resources, references and strategies that were discussed and shared by everyone in all of the workshops. The range of experiences, skills and expertise brought to each peer support meeting was rich and diverse, and the spirit in which this was shared and discussed was both encouraging and supportive. The depth of wisdom that was demonstrated untapped a rich source of enlightenment, learning and knowledge, and as the facilitators of these peer support meetings we also learned so much.

For those of you about to start on a journey of developing peer support systems in your schools . . .we wish you well.

Postscript

Appendix

Each session should last between 2 – 2½ hours unless the group agrees to leave out the professional development element of the meeting.

Suggested timetable for running a peer support meeting

10 minutes	Welcome the group. If this is a first meeting it may be appropriate to do a 'warm up' activity. Ground rules may need to be established. (See bibliography for resources.) If this is part of a series of meetings, the previous case study presenter may want the opportunity to share progress in relation to a particular pupil.
50 minutes	Professional development. The group facilitator may choose to use this time to work with the participants on specific areas of behaviour management. This could include work on identifying and assessing pupil behaviour as in Part One of this book or on one of the chapters in Part Two. It could be that the facilitator might want to use this time to go over the school's behaviour policy or introduce a topic such as assertive discipline. This is also a good time to share what is working well for individual members of the peer support group. It is also helpful to use this time to consider all the available resources and how they can be used to support agreed strategies to support pupils with emotional and behavioural difficulties. At all times the group facilitator should emphasise the importance that the work has on maximising teaching and learning. If appropriate, this should include a planned group activity.
10 minutes	Case study presentation and an opportunity to clarify particular issues.
5 minutes	The group should decide on the problem-solving technique to be used. The group facilitator should refresh memories about how the technique works.
1 hour	The group should either work as one, or in smaller groups, to generate a range of strategies to support the pupil and teaching staff using the agreed problem-solving technique.

	The group facilitator should ensure that an action plan is completed using the suggested pro forma on page 60.
15 minutes	Allow time for each group to feedback their discussions and specifically their action plan. Ensure that a consensus of a timetable for action is agreed, and that an appropriate member of the group has overall responsibility for its implementation, monitoring and evaluation. It is helpful to ensure that participants are aware of the range of resources or where to access this information to support them in implementing the action plan.

The group facilitator would be responsible for adapting the above times to suit the needs of any particular peer support meeting.

Bibliography

Ayers, H., Clarke, D., Murray, A. (1995) *Perspectives on Behaviour. A Practical Guide to Effective Interventions for Teachers.* London: David Fulton Publishers.

Ayers, H., Clarke, D., Ross, A. (1993) *Assessing Individual Needs. A Practical Approach.* London: David Fulton Publishers.

Balson, M. (1996) *Understanding Classroom Behaviour.* Hampshire: Arena/Ashgate Publishing.

Bernard, M. (1996) *You Can Do It! Student Guide.* Brighton: Anglo Scholarship Group.

Bond, T. (1990) *Games for Social and Life Skills.* Cheltenham: Stanley Thornes (first published by Hutchinson 1986).

Brandes, D. and Ginnis, P. (1986) *A Guide to Student-Centred Learning.* Oxford: Basil Blackwell Ltd.

Brandes, D. and Ginnis, P. (1990) *The Student-Centred School.* Oxford: Basil Blackwell Ltd.

Canter, L. and Canter, M. (1992) *Assertive Discipline. Positive Behaviour Management for Today's Classroom.* USA: Lee Canter and Associates.

Charles, C. M. (1996) *Building Classroom Discipline.* USA: Longman Publishers.

Creese, A., Daniels, H., Norwich, B. (1997) *Teacher Support Teams in Primary and Secondary Schools.* London: David Fulton Publishers.

Curry, M. and Bromfield, C. (1994) *Personal and Social Education for Primary Schools through Circle Time.* Stafford: NASEN Enterprises.

Department for Education and Employment (DfEE) (1997) *Excellence for all Children. Meeting Special Educational Needs.* London: The Stationery Office.

Department for Education and Employment (1998) *Meeting Special Educational Needs. A Programme of Action.* Sudbury: DfEE Publications Centre.

Department of Education and Science (DES) (1989) *Discipline in Schools, Report of the Committee of Enquiry chaired by Lord Elton.* London: HMSO.

Dinkmeyer, D., Dinkmeyer Jr, D., Sperry, L. (1987) *Adlerian Counselling and Psychotherapy.* USA: Macmillan Publishing.

Dreikurs, R. and Cassel, P. (1972) *Discipline Without Tears.* USA: Plume.

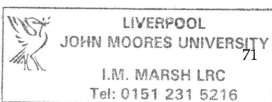

Dreikurs, R., Grunwald, B., Pepper, F. (1982) *Maintaining Sanity in the Classroom.* USA: Harper Collins.

East Devon Behaviour Support Team (1993) *Dealing with Problem Behaviour. A Booklet for Classroom Assistants.* Devon: Devon County Council.

Fullan, M. (1991) *The New Meaning of Educational Change.* London: Cassell.

Galvin, P. and Costa, P. (1992) *Developing a Behaviour Policy and Putting it into Practice.* Leeds: Leeds City Council.

Gill, D. and Monsen, J. (1996) 'The Staff Sharing Scheme', in Blyth, E. and Milner, J. (eds) *Exclusion from School.* London: Routledge.

Glasser, W. (1969) *Schools without Failure.* New York: Harper Row.

Gleiche, J. (1987) quoted in Woods, D. (ed.) *School Improvement Butterflies.* Birmingham LEA and The Questions Publishing Company.

Gordon, G. (1996) *Managing Challenging Children.* UK: Prim-Ed Publishing.

Gordon, T. (1970) *Parent Effectiveness Training.* New York: Plume.

Gordon, T. (1974) *Teacher Effectiveness Training.* New York: Peter H. Wyden.

Handy, C. (1994) *The Empty Raincoat.* London: Arrow Books.

Hanko, G. (1985) *Special Needs in Ordinary Classrooms. Supporting Teachers.* Oxford: Basil Blackwell.

Johnson, D. and Johnson, F. (1997) *Joining Together. Group Theory and Group Skills.* USA: Allyn and Bacon.

Jolly, M. and McNamara, E. (1992) *Towards Better Behaviour.* TBB, 7 Quinton Close, Ainsdale, Merseyside PR8 2TD.

Leeds Positive Behaviour Project (1992) *Managing the Difficult to Manage.* Leeds: Leeds City Council.

Lund, R. (1996) *A Whole-School Behaviour Policy. A Practical Guide.* London: Kogan Page.

MacGilchrist, B., Myers, K., Reed, J. (1997) *The Intelligent School.* London: Paul Chapman Publishing.

Millar, A. (1991) *Counselling Skills Sets A and B.* Cambridge: Daniels Publishing.

Murphy, E. (1992) *The Developing Child.* USA: Davies-Black.

New Outlooks Core Group (1998) *Behaviour in Schools: Framework for Intervention.* Birmingham: 'New Outlooks' Study of Emotional and Behavioural Problems for Birmingham City Council Education Department.

Porter, L. (1996) *Student Behaviour. Theory and Practice for Teachers.* Australia: Allen and Unwin.

Pratt, J. (1978) 'Stress inventory for teachers', in *Education Review* 30. New Zealand: Victoria University of Wellington/NZ Educational Institute.

Rogers, C. (1969) *Freedom to Learn.* Ohio: Charles E. Merrill.

Rogers, W. (1992) *Supporting Teachers in the Workplace.* Queensland: Jacaranda Press.

Rogers, W. (1993) *The Language of Discipline.* Plymouth: Northcote House.

Rogers, W. (1994) *Behaviour Recovery.* Essex: Longman.

Rogers, W. (1997) *Cracking the Hard Class.* Australia: Scholastic.

Sammons, P., Hillman, J., Mortimore, P. (1995) *Key Characteristics of Effective Schools: A Review of School Effectiveness Research.* London: OFSTED and Institute of London.

Index

Printed in the United Kingdom
by Lightning Source UK Ltd.
103733UKS00001B/163-170

9 781853 466199